LOVE AND LAUGHTER

WITH SPIRIT

MEET THE MEDIUM

LORAINE REES

by

Dr. Mary Ross

Loraine conducts a medium demonstration at the Mind Body Soul
Exhibition at the Kempton Park Racecourse, March 2010.

LOVE AND LAUGHTER

WITH SPIRIT

Meet the Medium

Loraine Rees

by

Dr. Mary Ross

Published by Lulu Press Inc.
Edited by: Virginia Heiner
Cover and text design: M. Ross

Photos by M. Ross
and from the private collection of Loraine Rees

ISBN 978-1-4467-9842-3

For more information on Loraine Rees contact:
www.LoraineReesMedium.com

To contact the author go to:
www.MaryRoss.com

To order copies of this book contact Loraine Rees,
Lulu Press, or www.MaryRoss.com

For my family

The author Dr. Mary Ross (left) with Loraine Rees.

ACKNOWLEDGEMENTS

This book could not have been possible without Loraine's generosity in sharing her insights, not only with me, but with anyone open to listening. It has been a real challenge keeping up with her, and a unique experience to observe her work and contribute in this small way to the message she brings on the eternal nature of love.

Thanks to Virginia Heiner for editing the text, Nancy Fraser for cover advice, Saavik Rai for computer expertise, and to Sue Bohane for content feedback, operating the video camera, and general support for the project. A special thanks to Cobham Cameras for lending me the video camera, and a big acknowledgment to my writing group.

I am pleased to thank all the people who so generously shared their experiences and thoughts about their readings with me. This book is a tribute to every one of them and the unbreakable bonds of love that stretch so much farther than the eye can see or the arms can reach. – M.R.

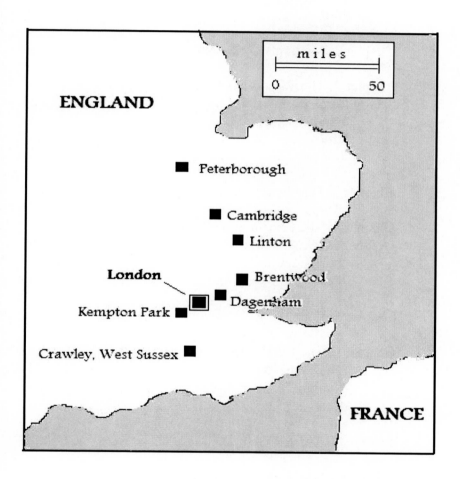

Locations from the text including sites of Loraine's shows.

CONTENTS

INTRODUCTION

Charlotte arrives at the psychic fair, not knowing what to expect. Her friend Anna has told her that she really should check out a medium named Loraine Rees. Charlotte has never done this kind of thing before, and isn't sure her husband, Peter, would approve. But he's not home and frankly, she's fed up waiting for him to return from his endless business trips.

At the psychic fair, Charlotte finds Loraine's booth and sits down for a reading.

"I'm sorry to tell you this," says Loraine, "but your husband is having an affair."

"No way!" says Charlotte, although even as she says it, part of her knows it would explain a lot. "Who is she?"

Loraine shakes her head. "It's not a 'she', it's a 'he'."

Charlotte doesn't believe it. Not Peter. He's her own husband; she knows him better than that. *Medium, schmedium!* Charlotte thinks at least she got a good laugh for her forty pounds.

That night, Peter returns from his business trip, exhausted. He drops his jacket on the couch and heads for the bath. A while later, out in the living room, the mobile phone in his jacket pocket starts to ring. Charlotte answers for him. A man asks to speak with Peter.

"He's in the bath," she tells the caller. "Do you want me to bring the phone in there to him?"

"Don't do that!" says the caller. "You can't go into the bathroom with my boyfriend in there!"

Charlotte's story really happened. Everything you will read in these pages is true. This book is an account of my interviews and observations of the clairvoyant medium Loraine Rees at work, backed-up by tape recordings (and one video recording), as well as follow-up interviews with people who have received readings. In some places I have changed the names, but the events, situations, and exchanges reported here are entirely and astonishingly true.

Loraine Rees is a rarity. Not only is her accuracy rate very high, but the messages she delivers are infused with her healthy sense of humour. The purpose of this book is to provide a glimpse into Loraine's work and her special gift, and to share the simple but powerful underlying message that comes through with every reading she does, about the unbreakable strength of the bonds of love.

For those already familiar with her work, this book aims to examine her process and address some questions you might have for her yourself. If you are not familiar with her work, this book attempts to give you a small taste of what she does.

Some of the contents of this book might be hard to believe. There are things that have happened during Loraine's shows that I might have had a hard time believing myself, if I hadn't been there to see and hear them in person. And while I have a creative mind, many of the incidences reported here are beyond my imagination; I could not have made them up if I tried.

I have gone over my tapes again and again to make sure what is reported here is accurate, and that everything happened just as I portray it. If you have doubts of the authenticity of the events in this book, here's a simple thing you can do yourself to help you make up your mind. Go to any of the events, shows, or Mind Body Soul Exhibitions where she will be conducting private readings. You can find her schedule on her web site (www.LoraineReesMedium.com). When you get to the event, walk around the aisles and check out the mediums and clairvoyants who are scheduling readings. Have a glance at their sign-up sheets. Many will have plenty of available spaces on their schedules and might try to coax you in for a reading. But even though Loraine Rees is not a "celebrity psychic" that advertises her readings of famous people, or promotes herself on TV or hardly anywhere else, unless you arrive very early in the day, most of her bookings will already be filled. That's because her word-of-mouth reputation is so strong. Her bookings get taken up very fast, and it is all due to people telling their friends that they really should go see her. Some mediums leave the shows early, due to lack of clients. But Loraine is booked solid every minute of those events she attends, often with people hovering around her booth, just hoping for a cancellation. If you go to one of her events and find this is not the case, I invite you to write to me at *LoraineReesBook@aol.com* and I will promptly send the price of this book to the charity of your choice.

Whether you are a sceptic, a believer, or a little of both, I hope you enjoy this tiny window into the life and work of a very busy medium.

Chapter 1

MEDIUMS – WHY NOT?

Before I met Loraine, I was intrigued but sceptical, in large part because there are so many psychics out there who are happy to take your money but give you little in return. Believe me, I have seen my share of phoneys. Have you had an experience with a fake psychic that went anything like this?

I duck under the rainbow-coloured curtains to enter the semi-private booth of Shezra, "Medium to the Stars." Her hair, jet black, brushes down onto the shoulders of her long purple velvet dress. Her smile is a garish swath of red glitter paint, and having read somewhere that the average woman consumes two tubes of lipstick each year, I can't help but wonder where all those sparkles end up.

"Come in," she says in an eerie voice, taking my hand. "I am Shezra."

Behind her on the wall is a large airbrushed photo of her, this time as a platinum blonde, with the caption, "As seen on TV."

Shezra lets go of my left hand, with my well-worn wedding band, and she says, "I can see that you are in an established relationship. How long have you been together?"

I tell her the number of years.

"Very good," says Shezra. "Please be seated."

I sit across a small table from her, trying to get comfortable. It's my first time to see her, and I don't know what to expect. I am hoping Shezra is genuine, and am trying hard to keep an open mind.

She closes her eyes, as if in a trance. Then she says, "I can see that you're very..." Her eyes open ever so slightly as she looks down and sees my pink socks, which don't quite match my green striped shirt. "...Creative."

She's reading my clothes, not anything else, and in my mind, I see a parade of chai tea lattes, the exact number of these foaming creations I could have treated myself to if I hadn't spent my forty pounds on this twenty minutes of Shezra's time.

"Well?" Shezra asks. She seems annoyed. I'm not sure why. Is it my turn to speak? Aren't I paying *her* to read *me*?

She clears her throat, and repeats, "I SAID, you are very... CREATIVE?"

"Okay."

"Okay?" she snaps. " 'Okay' is not a proper response. It's not polite. I need more than 'okay,' I need a proper response from you. Look, I'm trying to give you a good reading, but I can't if you refuse to answer appropriately."

"What is an appropriate response?" I ask.

"You may say 'yes'," Shezra informs me. "Not 'yeah,' not 'okay,' but 'yes.' Alternatively, you may say, 'I don't understand.' Do you understand?"

"Yes, I understand." Oops. I've mixed up the replies, and this wasn't one of the officially sanctioned responses. I try to smile my way out of it, but Shezra is not amused, and I am feeling like I'm back in school, invoking the teacher's wrath for my wrong answer. And I have paid for this privilege?

Then Shezra looks into her crystal ball and says, "I see a house. And children. I'm not sure if they're yours. Do you have children?"

"Yes," I answer dutifully.

"More than one?"

Another affirmative.

"Less than five?" she asks, watching my eyes. "Less than four?"

Yes, again.

"Ah, I see the children are yours. I see two. There may be a third but..."

I look confused.

"... but the third one is not yours. Perhaps a niece or nephew. Or a friend's child."

I am *so* not impressed. I check my watch as discreetly as I can.

"I see an older woman in the world beyond," she tells me. "Perhaps your mother. Or your grandmother. Is your mother still on the earth plane?"

I tell her that she is.

"Then it must be your grandmother. Or perhaps your husband's grandmother?"

I don't respond because I know it wouldn't be appreciated, to tell her that my husband's grandmother, at ninety-five, is still working a nine-hour work day when she's not off cruising the Mediterranean.

"This woman," Shezra continues, "is telling me that your mother was in the military. During a war. I'm seeing her in a uniform."

My mother was not military, she was a social worker, and she didn't wear a uniform. I respond the only way I'm allowed. "I don't understand."

Shezra frowns. "Then perhaps she helped in the war effort. Maybe she worked at a factory where they made parts for the soldiers. As a nurse. Or as a volunteer. Some type of support function."

My mother never worked in a factory and practically faints at the sight of a needle. In her youth, at a time when almost everyone else supported the war, my mother was so opposed to violence that she served as a reference for the very unpopular conscientious objectors.

I know she won't like it, but I have no choice but to say, "I don't understand."

Shezra's eyes flash. "What do you mean, you don't understand? What's the problem? After all, this is YOUR reading.

This is YOUR family we are talking about. How can you fail to understand your own life?"

This is not what I had in mind when I entered her booth. Could it be that she's just having a bad day? But, as I avert my eyes from her ire and frustration, I notice her sign-up sheet, with two dozen available spaces, is quite empty. In this massive convention hall, packed with believers and hopefuls, I am only the fifth person of the day to book a reading with Shezra. That means her previous four customers on this day have not recommended her to their friends. This, on top of everything else, makes me wonder. Are they all scam artists? Is there anyone who is for real? Is it possible that there are people who can truly connect in ways that are closed to the rest of us?

I stopped wondering in March of 2007, within eighteen seconds of a walk-in cold reading with Loraine Rees.

It was the Kensington Olympia Mind Body Soul Exhibition in London, and I had agreed to go and meet a friend there. I had never been to one of these events before but we decided to go see what it was all about. Perhaps it was my scientific curiosity that led me to go, the same curiosity that led to me to achieve a master's degree in earth science and a doctorate in tertiary education. I have always thought it is just as foolhearty to dismiss something because it makes you feel uncomfortable as it is to believe something without evidence.

The big draw of the exhibition weekend was a presentation by Colin Fry, from the television show "Sixth

Sense," and my friend and I had purchased advance tickets. Unfortunately, I arrived a few minutes late, after they had already closed the big double doors to his sold-out presentation.

Disappointed that I had lost my chance to see the famous celebrity psychic, I wandered through the exhibition halls, now depressingly quiet with so many people off in the big auditorium watching Colin Fry.

As I walked by the stalls selling crystals, reflexology oils, and computerized astrology readings, I stopped at the booth of a medium. There was nothing particularly remarkable about her, no Guinevere dress or day-glow lipstick, and no posters with rave reviews. She was just a normal-looking woman, like someone you might see at the grocery store, sitting down at a card table. She didn't coax me to join her or hound me as some of the other vendors had done when I walked by. She had no flashy advertising, and no publicity except a couple of little fliers run off on a copy machine. But for some reason, I decided to sit down, even though I fully expected to be unimpressed, with a dismal substitute for missing the big celebrity psychic.

What a pleasure to be wrong. After asking my maiden name and holding an object that I owned, Loraine was off and running, the words coming out without pause or preamble.

"Your father is here," she said. "He looks like you, and he died of cancer." That was true enough. My father, Earl, had passed away two years before, of stomach cancer. Of all his children, I was the only one who looked like him.

Without stopping, Loraine continued. "The younger man is here, too. He also died of cancer. His was liver cancer, and he says he turned so yellow at the end that he looked like the evil monster in a movie."

This time, there was no "I don't understand" about it, because the younger man on the other side was my good friend James, who had died the previous month of liver cancer, and had gone so yellow that in his last days of consciousness, someone had thoughtlessly told him that he looked like the evil emperor in Star Wars. It still boggles my mind that someone would say this to a dying person. Even stranger, how could Loraine have possibly known? It was a very specific detail, and I hadn't told her anything except my maiden name. There was no fishing for clues or asking loaded questions, it just came out in the first few seconds of the reading.

It went on from there as for the next twenty minutes, I wrote madly, trying to jot down everything she said, barely able to keep up. And as I listened, I realized it was more than the facts and details that she was relating about my relatives and friends that had crossed over. It was also the essence of their personalities that came through, with their distinct types of humour intact. Loraine related conversations and specific experiences of my friends and relatives, including things I hadn't known myself and later found out to be true.

Loraine also mentioned a baby girl. I immediately thought of the baby a friend just had. But that baby was a little boy so I was confused by the reference. It wasn't until I listened to the tape three days later that I realized Loraine had been talking about a little girl on the spirit side, a child who had already crossed over. Then it made sense as I had a daughter years ago who died very young.

At one point during that reading, Loraine said, "You're a writer. I think you're the one that should write my book."

By the end of that reading, I knew two things: Loraine was different from every other clairvoyant I had ever met, and she didn't have to ask me twice about writing her story.

It didn't happen right away. But over the next few years, I was able to catch up with her again, document a number of her shows, and interview people who received readings. And every session has been a profound experience as I have found myself impressed all over again, with every encounter, by Loraine's accuracy, her generosity of spirit, and her ability to connect people with loved ones they thought they had lost.

But it isn't easy trying to keep up with Loraine's schedule. She does up to two hundred readings a week, all booked without publicity but entirely referred by word of mouth. Unlike Shezra, Loraine books up very fast, so you have to be quick to get in to see her.

Writing this book has been quite an experience for me, as it has allowed me to explore Loraine's work, and ask her questions in greater depth than she typically has time to discuss when she's doing a reading or a show. It has been a real pleasure to observe this "psychic telephone" to the other side, and watch the awe on people's faces when they receive special messages from someone they thought they would never hear from again. This project has also allowed me to ask her how she does it, and what she has learned from it all.

I am pleased to present this account, as I have come to believe that Loraine's second sight, or inner sight, is a rare and precious gift. But don't take it from me. Judge for yourself. Read on, and see what you think.

Chapter 2

THE WEST SUSSEX SHOW
NOVEMBER 2008
Seeing Loraine's Show For The First Time

It's a cold wet Sunday in November at the 2008 Psychic, Crafts and Holistic Show in the West Sussex town of Crawley. I squeeze through the milling crowds of people checking out the stalls and vendors, and the largest assortment of crystals I've ever seen.

Threading my way through the hall, I find the demonstration hall on the far right, a rectangular room with about one hundred and fifty chairs. I select a chair up near the front, my tape recorder ready and waiting. It has been almost a year since I had my private reading with Loraine, and I have never seen one of her shows. This is my first time to attend, and I have no idea how she will deal with a whole room full of people. I don't know what to expect, but I'm ready to record it all.

The room fills up quickly. By the time Loraine arrives, almost every chair is taken. In black jeans and stiletto leather boots, she walks down the centre aisle towards the front. She carries a bottle of water, but other than that, she has no props, no microphone, and is armed with nothing but a smile.

"Can someone shut the door?" she asks. A woman near the back complies and Loraine continues, "Thanks. Can you all hear me at the back? I'm finding it a bit hard to shout today. Usually I don't have trouble shouting, but today I'm fighting a cold. Has anyone seen me before?"

A few people nod.

"Good. Can we all be really happy today, because with this miserable cold, I'm feeling like shit."

Loraine shrugs sheepishly as she notices a baby in a pram staring up at her. Several people giggle.

"Yeah, you know it. You're probably thinking she might not be a good clairvoyant, but she's good on stage."

Lots of good-natured laughter.

"When I come to you, all I want is your name, okay? Now, can everyone uncross your legs?"

People straighten their legs.

"That's better. Because my spirit guide, Ramos, likes to look up the ladies' skirts."

This gets a laugh.

"Actually," she explains, "it's so your energy is open to the process. Are we ready?"

I look around and notice people smiling. From my reading, I knew she was good with one-to-one readings. I had no idea she was also a comedienne. With the mood lightened, people are relaxed and eager to see what's going to happen next. Loraine has warmed up this room of strangers in less than a minute. Now it's time for business as she walks up the aisle.

"When I come to you, what do I want?" she asks.

A muffled chorus says, "Our names."

"That's right. And do speak up nice and clear, because we're all a nosey bunch here and we all want to know all your gossip. But if I'm getting too close to the mark and you don't want anyone else to know, just..." she makes a slicing motion, "go like this. Okay? But I talk really fast, so chances are, I've probably already said it."

HEATHER

As Loraine searches the crowd, she narrows in on a blonde fiftyish woman near the front.

"I'm drawn here so I'm going to come straight to you. Hello darlin'. What's your name?"

The woman responds, "Heather."

"Hello, Heather. I've got your mum's mum here. Do you remember your grandma, because she stands right there with you."

Heather nods.

"She says she's got a birthday coming up, because she's giving me memories of a birthday. Do you understand that?"

Another confirmation.

"Who's been having trouble with their back? I don't know who's having trouble with their back, but I get the feeling that my back is bloody killing me. Does this make sense?"

It does.

"She's also telling me about rock and roll. Somebody used to like to do the jive and the twist."

Heather giggles. "That was me."

"She's also showing me somebody flipping their knickers off at you, you know what I mean?"

Heather grins mischievously.

"She's got a lot to say about that, but she's having a good old chuckle about it. There's also talk of a move. Somebody wants to move, and it's almost like this move is going to be delayed. I don't think it's you, but it's someone around you, your nan [grandmother] is telling me. Oh, and I've got your dad here."

Heather nods.

"He comes in and gives you a big hello. And he tells me his feet used to kill him. He had terrible trouble with his feet."

"He certainly did."

"But now he's running around, and he's got all the nurses chasing around after him up there. Typical me, he says. I'm also picking up two birthdays next to each other. Two birthdays very close to each other. Do you understand that?"

Heather agrees that she does.

"And there's something do to with coloured ribbons. Blue and white. And I don't know who used to make rosettes. Blue and white rosettes made out of ribbons."

Heather looks confused.

"I don't know who is was that made rosettes out of blue and white ribbons, but can you hold on to that? I think you need to look back a bit on Dad's side of the family for that."

Heather says that she will.

"And your dad's telling me that he loves you and misses you. He's also giving me a connection with America. I don't know if you're going to America on holiday."

Again, confirmation.

"He tells me that he's coming with you, and you don't even have to pay for him. What happened to his money by the way?"

"I don't know."

"Of course you don't. And he says he doesn't know, either. He's sure they bloody well spent it. He was tight at times, wasn't he? But he liked to keep a few bob in his back pocket."

"Yes, he did."

"Where was Dad from?"

Heather says her father was from Scotland.

Loraine nods. "That explains it. He has such a strong accent, and he talks so quick it's hard for me to keep up. And there's someone there named John. Do you know who John is?"

Heather nods.

"And Jimmy's there with them, too."

Recognising the name, Heather nods again.

"There's also a connection with twins. One lived and one passed."

Heather doesn't understand this one.

"And Agnes. Who's Agie?"

Heather doesn't answer. A dark-haired young women beside Heather whispers something to her. Heather looks surprised, then says, "Oh, yes!"

"And someone's having trouble with their throat. Someone's putting Vicks around their chest."

"My dad did that."

Loraine starts to writhe. "Oh my, he's doing it to me! Putting Vicks on my chest and.. what's this? His hands are moving further down? What... Don't try that with me!"

The whole room erupts in good-natured laughter.

"He's having a good old giggle with me. Your dad was very nice, wasn't he? And someone died of a heart attack. He went very quickly, very suddenly. He used to wear a cap on his head. He's with your dad."

Heather looks confused.

"The name George is given to me."

"Oh, yes. George. His heart went."

"And somebody got chucked to Australia. I think he was a bit of a naughty boy back then. Because I do feel he had to go, and the family lost contact. Because Dad tells me sometimes what you don't know can't hurt you. But he tells me that you had a cousin, and he had no bloody choice but to go."

"That was cousin George."

"And he got someone in a pudding [pregnant]. Dad says we find out a lot more about what went on once we get up here. And there's someone here named Betty. Do you understand that?"

"Yes."

"Where's your daughter?"

Heather points to the young brunette beside her. "Right here."

"Thank you. She doesn't look anything like you, does she? Well, your grandad's glad to see you. He says you're doing just fine."

The daughter smiles.

"And someone's got a basement full of Teddy bears. A basement full of cuddly toys."

Heather doesn't respond. Loraine presses the issue. "Who's got the cuddly toys?"

Heather says, "I do have a lot of toys."

"What kind of toys."

Heather hangs her head, embarrassed she's been caught out. "Teddy bears."

The audience roars.

Who's Ali or Alison? Do you understand who she is?"

"Yes."

"And someone's getting married, because your dad's showing me a wedding. Do you understand?"

Heather nods.

"And your dad says we're all coming to the wedding and we won't cost a bloody penny. But your dad loves you and misses you loads. And with that I'll say God bless and thank you."

As Loraine walks away, Heather and her daughter are both smiling, although Heather is still a little pink-faced about the Teddy bears.

There's a hushed anticipation, with all eyes on Loraine as the crowd wonders who she will come to next.

She puts her hands on her hips. "You know, you can clap."

The audience erupts in applause.

Loraine coughs, then takes a sip of water. "Actually, I'm dying here, really. I have this terrible cold, and was going to cancel, but you know what my husband said? Just do it. Where is he? Is he here? No? He's disappeared? Well, I'm not surprised. You know what it is? I'll bet he's thinking a year being married to me is probably enough."

People laugh, enjoying the fact that she doesn't take herself too seriously.

This is the first reading I've seen Loraine do for someone else, in a public venue, and I have not yet figured out what I think of it. Some of it felt a bit generic. For a woman of Heather's age, it's anyone's guess that her grandmother and perhaps her father may have already crossed over. Going to America on holiday is not terribly unique, nor is having a wedding to attend. And there were the two items, the twin connection and the blue and white rosettes, that Heather couldn't validate.

But the number of names -- John, Jimmy, Agnes, Betty, and Alison -- all of them part of Heather's circle of family and friends, is harder to dismiss. I also have Scottish ancestry, but most of those names wouldn't resonate with me at all.

Then there was the cousin sent away to Australia, a rather specific detail, and the problems with his feet that Heather's father endured.

But for me, my favourite part of the reading was the reference to the Teddy bears, an addiction Heather really didn't want to admit, but was forced to when Loraine persisted.

I look around and gauge the mood in the room. Does the audience seem impressed? A bit. Perhaps not yet entirely sold, but many seem to be considering there may be something to this.

And are they enjoying themselves? Absolutely! I notice that the people have shifted, leaning forward now, eager to see what she's going to do next.

BROO

From the right side of the room, Loraine reads a middle-aged woman named Broo. Loraine "gets" that Broo's mother and aunt have passed away and that Broo is giving up cooking the Christmas feast this year. Loraine asks Broo if her father died from emphysema around September. Broo explains that he died in August, and it was someone else who died from the emphysema.

Loraine asks Broo if she is a writer working on a love story that is a little bit raunchy. Broo confirms she is writing a steamy romance novel.

Loraine is delighted. "I'd like to read that. Although for me, after six kids, I guess I've seen it all. Six kids but only one orgasm. Pretty good, eh? I eloped, you know. Oh yes, up in Scotland. I'll bet he regrets it now, my husband. My poor third husband."

The audience roars. A young man in the second row smiles. Loraine notices him.

"Want to be the fourth?" Loraine says with a devilish grin. "Why not?" she adds. "Wouldn't you like to catch my cold in a moment of truth? You know, I could get another divorce. They've gone down in price. They used to be expensive, but now you can do it on the internet for thirty-nine quid. That's right, instant divorce. All you do is turn on the computer."

The audience giggles, knowing this is not that far from the truth.

Loraine returns to Broo and advises her to fix her back window. Loraine says that Broo's father is worried about the way it doesn't shut properly, and wants Broo to take care of it before someone breaks in and robs her. Broo admits the back window isn't closing all the way, and assures Loraine that she will get it fixed.

The audience applauds.

"Sorry if I'm not as bubbly as I usually am," Loraine tells the audience. "Do you think I'm flat today?"

Several people murmur, "No."

Loraine takes another sip of water and shakes her head. "Just do it, he says."

An older woman smiles up at Loraine, revealing several missing teeth. At that moment, Loraine's husband Mark enters the back of the room. Loraine notices him. The older woman follows her gaze.

"Mark," Loraine calls out. "I think this woman wants to have a go at you."

The older woman giggles.

Loraine pats the older woman on the shoulder. "Hello, darlin'. You're my new friend, aren't you?"

The woman nods, pleased.

"I haven't got many friends," Loraine admits. "It's a shame, but clairvoyants lead a lonely life. It's true. We only talk to dead people."

Her joke gets a good response as Loraine continues up the aisle.

JOHN

"I'm seeing lots of lights here," Loraine says, "so I'm not sure where to go. But I think I'm being drawn to…" Loraine stops by a gentleman in a dark blue zip fleece. "Hello. What's your name?"

"John," he replies.

"Hi, John, how are you? Your dad's here. He was a lovely man. What's going on with your telly?"

"It keeps turning off."

"Your dad says don't bother to get a new one. He says the problem with it is him. He's just making contact. He also says you've got a native American spirit guide. And your mum's mum is here. She loved to make dumplings."

"She did."

"She had a son who died and she never got over his death. She had two sons who went to war. One came back but the other one died over there."

"Absolutely true."

"And Arthur, that's the name I'm getting. Your uncle Arthur. He's another spirit guide. He says he died fighting for his country and he didn't get jack shit."

"Right. We called him Uncle Ted."

"But he says there are medals for him somewhere, and you can go collect them, if you want a mission."

John's eyes light up. "I will."

"And I'm seeing a sewing machine. And your mother. The name Dorothy is given to me."

John confirms that Dorothy was his mother's name.

"Your mother is making curtains, so I don't know if that means you're going to be changing your curtains."

"We are."

"Thank you. And I'm getting the name Rosie. And the name George. Do those names mean anything to you?"

John nods.

"Your uncle who died in the war, he sends his love. So I'll leave you with that, and God bless. Thank you."

"Thank *you*," John replies, beaming.

Loraine walks down the aisle.

"Now, where am I drawn to next? I've got lights in this area. Let's see... so many lights. It looks like I've got more dead people at my show than live ones."

People enjoy the joke, but in truth, the room is actually packed to capacity. Then Loraine apologizes again for not being as bubbly as usual. It is hard for me to imagine anyone being even more animated and engaging.

Before the hour is up, Loraine reads five more people, and the bulk of what she says is quickly confirmed. If I had been leaning on the fence when I walked in, her accuracy in this show would have nudged me over towards the believer side. I am impressed not only with her readings but with her self-depreciating humour and the way she has delighted the audience.

But how do the people who received a public reading feel about it? After the show, I am able to catch up with John and his wife Joyce to talk to them about the experience. Although his reading was rather short, I am curious to see how he felt about it.

"She was spot on about so many things," John tells me. "When I was very young, my uncle Arthur, who we called Ted, went to war. Before he went off, he held me and said goodbye to me. I was just a baby. He died in that war and never came back. Somehow he must have known he might not come back because he wrote me a letter. I didn't know about the letter for many years because my dad kept it back and only gave it to me when I turned eighteen. So for Loraine to bring up my uncle Ted brought home a very real thing to me."

Joyce concurs. "It was very special to hear from John's uncle."

"The family all came through," says John. "It was marvellous. We didn't know much about George and that side of the family because there was a quarrel. After the argument, Mum wasn't very popular with her side of the family and didn't get a lot of affection, and that has always been a big worry to me. But to see them linked now and coming through together is just marvellous. I have felt that my father was around, but to hear it confirmed was just lovely."

Joyce adds, "And Loraine was right about the telly. It keeps going off all the time. Someone said maybe it's because the system is swapping over from analogue to digital, but that's not the problem. It just turns itself off. I'm glad we don't need a new telly. But if he's going to keep doing that, I wish he would go ahead and fix the remote because it won't work."

It's a funny idea, spirits fixing your electronics, and we enjoy a good laugh. I've heard stories before of lights and TVs going off and on after a death, but never a remote control or a gadget being repaired. Too bad it doesn't seem to work that way.

John continues. "It's interesting that my dad came through because when he was alive, he didn't believe in any of this. He would turn his back on it. He would sit on his stool and turn the other way. He was a lovely chap with a good sense of humour, a lecturer with his own beliefs. But he thought anything to do with clairvoyance was just psychology. I've often wondered and worried about him because of his lack of belief. But to hear from him that he's all right is just lovely."

Joyce agrees. Then John sums up his final thoughts about the reading. "I was one of three boys, and of all the brothers, I was the only one that Uncle Ted knew. So, for him to confirm that he's been looking over me all these years, well, that's what it's all about, isn't it?"

I am awed by how much the reading has meant to John, and the way it has resolved so many deep-seated issues for him, from his mother's rift with her family, his father's lack of belief, to his special bond with an uncle he barely met. Watching a person being read, nodding his head and agreeing or disagreeing, gives a sense of Loraine's accuracy, but sometimes it falls short of explaining the significance or impact a message might have. I realize that John's summation of the reading has hit the nail on the head -- family, taking care of family, and not letting *anything* get in the way of that. Wise words, indeed.

Loraine's words have touched John's soul. How did she know exactly what to say? How does she do it? Where does it come from? To consider this, let's go back to the beginning, when Loraine first discovered her abilities.

Chapter 3

DISCOVERING HER GIFT

Loraine was born in Dagenham, east of London, in 1963. Her father, Henry, drove a lorry while her mother, Maureen, was a nurse. Loraine was their first child with baby Paul arriving two years later.

Loraine's first memory is as a child of four years old. Her mum and dad brought her, along with her baby brother, on a trip to the sea.

As they walked along the seafront of a little town, they got lost. They had never been in the town before, and by this time, they were very far from their car. Loraine's mother tried to hide her worry as she pushed the pram with one arm and held Loraine's hand in the other. But even so, Loraine knew there was something wrong as they walked and walked for what seemed like miles.

All of a sudden, Loraine realized she was not lost at all. Pointing ahead, she said, "Right there! It's the big white house where I used to live before you were my mum and dad."

They didn't believe her. They hadn't been this way before, so there was no way to know what was up ahead.

But Loraine knew better. "That's where I go. To the big willow tree."

Then they turned a corner, and right there was a large old white house, and to the right was a sprawling willow.

As they stopped at the tree to rest, Loraine sat on a low branch and could see familiar patterns in the bark. They looked like faces – the faces of old friends.

Although Loraine was only four, that image has stayed with her to this day. Because even at that tender age, it made her realize that there were worlds beyond what others could see. But these worlds were very clear to her.

The gift of having psychic abilities was not that unusual in Loraine's family as it had been passed down through the genes for generations on her mother's side, from a long line of Irish gypsies. While the psychic abilities were most often expressed in the women, the men enjoyed other pursuits, including bare-fisted fighting. In the 1870's in the Irish town of Limerick, Loraine's great-great-grandfather's brother, Patrick Brown, accidentally killed an opponent during a fight. To avoid persecution, he fled to Yorkshire along with several members of the family.

Loraine's great-grandmother, Lucy Emelia Brown, moved with them and obtained domestic work in the household of a British major. But although Lucy Emelia was a religious woman, she had a child out of wedlock and her infant daughter, Joyce Brown, was put into St. Bernardo's home for orphans.

But Lucy Emelia didn't forget about her child. For years she saved her money diligently, and when Joyce was twelve, Lucy Emelia appeared at the orphanage and asked to see Joyce.

"Who are you?" Joyce asked.

"I'm your mother, and I'm here to take you home."

"No, you're not," said Joyce. "I don't have a mother."

Lucy Emelia wrapped the girl in a warm coat and took her to London where she had rented a room, so the two of them could finally be a family.

But Joyce wasn't having any of it, and resented her mother for springing such a surprise on her.

Unfortunately, their relationship never blossomed. At seventeen, Joyce ran away with a boyfriend, was married by nineteen, and soon gave birth to Maureen, Loraine's mother.

Loraine learned all this family history from her great-grandmother Lucy Emelia. As a child, Loraine often had delightful conversations with her great-grandmother. As with many families, she shared a special relationship with her elder, and listened with rapt attention as she learned about the family history.

From these conversations, Loraine also learned how her great-grandfather, named Tom, was one of the first men to drive a steam train through Yorkshire, servicing the cities of Newcastle and Leeds.

Loraine didn't question what Lucy Emelia told her, as most children don't question what their grandparents tell them.

But in her case, it was different because Lucy Emelia had died twenty years before Loraine was born.

When Loraine's mother, Maureen, found out what Loraine had learned, she verified it was all true. Maureen realized by then that Loraine had "the gift," and knew that when Loraine talked about her "play friends," that Loraine was not referring to the typical childhood imaginary friends but to friendly spirits who had departed.

Maureen herself had spent many hours of her own childhood "talking" to spirits that visited her. Maureen's aunt Jesse Brown had become a well-known medium, so it wasn't unusual for the girls in the family to have a connection with the other side. But in Maureen's case, as she grew up, she didn't choose to develop these skills. Instead, she became a nurse and married Henry, a truck driver with no known psychic talent in his family history.

But Henry had some psychic talent as well, and although he couldn't communicate with the other side, he could often sense when a spirit was nearby.

Between the two of them, it was likely that their daughter, Loraine, would have at least a touch of the gift.

When Loraine was about five, her parents decided to buy a house in Dagenham for their growing family. They were tired of paying rent, and were pleased when a house came on the market that they could afford.

Maureen took young Loraine to go see the house. But when they arrived, Loraine refused to go in. Instead, she stood outside, screaming, "Look! Look! There's a man, and he's bleeding!"

Loraine's mum tried to convince her there was no one there. But Loraine was adamant, and wouldn't go any closer.

A neighbour came by and asked Maureen if she was going to buy the house.

"Buy it?" said Maureen. "I can't even get my little girl to go in it. She says there's a man in there."

The neighbour looked in, no man in sight, but her curiosity was piqued. "Where did she see the man?"

Maureen pointed to the place inside the house that had terrified Loraine.

Then the neighbour explained. "That's where the old boy fell to his death." Apparently, the previous owner, an older gentleman, had died right where Loraine saw the bleeding man.

They never did buy that house. But it reconfirmed to Loraine's mother that Loraine's psychic connection with the spirit world was already very strong.

As a child, Loraine felt her gift was quite normal because she had always had it, from as far back as she could remember. As some people can play a musical instrument by ear just by "listening" to the notes in their head, Loraine could always articulate messages that she "hears" in her head. It never felt strange to her or intruded on her daily life in a negative way. However, by the time she was about eight, she knew that her friends couldn't see what she saw, and might not understand. So for the most part, she learned to keep her connection to the spirit world to herself.

It wasn't hard. Even as a young child, she was able to separate the psychic world from the physical world when she wanted to immerse herself in the real world of childhood.

However, when she reached the age when young girls start to notice the boys, and her friends would huddle together to ask if a particular boy might be interested, Loraine was ready with an answer.

"Sam's not going to ask you out, but Steve will."

Her ability to guide her friends towards receptive dates made her very popular amongst her peers. They didn't bother to ask how she knew, and she didn't offer to explain.

Around this time, she realised that she could see images in fires. Her house had a gas fireplace and she would sometimes notice things in the flames that no one else could see.

One day in school, in the science lab with her best friend Alison, the two girls were assigned a frog to dissect. Annoyed with that prospect, Loraine fidgeted with the lab's Bunsen burner and turned on the gas. As it ignited, she saw something in the blue flames that shocked her.

Without thinking, Loraine turned to her friend and blurted out, "Alison, your mother's dead."

"No, she's not," said Alison. "She's in the hospital, but she's getting better. She'll be all right."

Alison didn't come to school the next day. Or the next. It was three weeks before Loraine saw her again, because Alison's mother had indeed passed away.

When Alison finally returned to school, the girls resumed their friendship. But the experience taught Loraine to be more careful when sharing information, and from then on, she tried to become more tactful in her delivery.

Still, during a reading, the information comes to Loraine very fast – so fast that it is hard to keep up with it all. That's why Loraine records her private readings on tape, so the person being read can review the tape later, as needed, to have the chance to consider everything that she says, and pick up the bits that might have been missed in the information overload. I know that with my first reading, that tape was invaluable. Loraine picked up on several things I had not even known about, including information about my great-aunt Peggy, whom I remember only vaguely. But when I checked with my older sister, I discovered the details Loraine gave me, that she never married, were true.

Some people find the speed of Loraine's delivery unnerving. There are no long pauses to catch your breath. Loraine speaks very fast, and as she explains it, her spirit guides don't need to work that hard with her. When she wants to hear it, the information just comes, in a steady stream, without any fuss or pause.

After seeing Loraine in action, I made plans to document her next show.

But a week before the date, Loraine suffered a difficult miscarriage, and had to cancel. In the hospital, they had a hard time controlling her bleeding and for a long time, her medical condition did became even worse. Weakened by the loss of blood, she caught an infection that spread dangerously through her chest until it invaded her lungs. Then her heart stopped. For seven minutes she was clinically dead but they were finally able to revive her. Her heart stopped a second time and thankfully, they were able to revive her once again.

Both times, she recalls feeling herself in a tunnel of light, and being told by family members who had already departed that it wasn't her time, and that she had to go back.

After waking up in the hospital, it was a long slow battle back to good health. But when she regained her strength, it seemed that her connection to the other side had increased. As she explains it, although she has never been afraid of dying, the experience of touching the other side somehow made her more sensitive and compassionate to others. And with that, she found her contact with the other side had grown even stronger than before.

I wondered about that. To me, her inner perception already seemed remarkable. Could it get any stronger? As soon as she was well enough to return to her busy schedule, I was ready to find out.

Chapter 4

THE KENSINGTON OLYMPIA SHOW
October 2009

It has been nearly a year since I saw Loraine last, and I'm curious to see what's going to happen at her demonstration at the London Mind Body Soul Exhibition at the Kensington Olympia venue. I arrive early in the day, because in addition to documenting her show, I also want to get a private reading. I have learned by trial and error that if I arrive after 10:30 in the morning, her appointments for the day might already be gone. I am pleased that I have made it to her sign-up sheet in time to secure a booking for 5:20 p.m., one of her last appointments of the day.

Today Loraine has a one hour show scheduled upstairs at 3:45 in the afternoon. After a good wander around the stalls of the vendors, I arrive at the workshop room fifteen minutes early to get a seat in the front row on the far left side, where there is room to park my tape recorder. Loraine enters on time, and starts to warm up the room right away.

"Can everybody hear me? I'm Loraine. I've had six kids and three husbands, so I'm doing all right. Can you all uncross your legs for me? Now when I come to you, I want you to tell me your name, and answer yes or no. I don't want you to say anything else, or give me any clues. I work with my spirit guide, Ramos, and he doesn't need lots of clues. I'm not that good at picking them up anyway, so let's start. I'm seeing lots of lights all around the room. Plenty of lights here, so I think I will go to..."

JADE

Loraine walks up to a woman with light brown hair. "I think I'm with you. What's your name?"

The woman identifies herself as Jade.

"Hello, Jade. You know more dead people than I've had hot dinners. I do feel there's quite a few people around you. Do you remember your gran [grandmother]?"

"Yes."

"She's here to say hello. And can you take a young girl, a teenager or a girl in her early twenties who has passed?"

Jade nods.

"I do feel she's passed a few years now. She's sobbing her eyes out. She just wants to say... are you her mum? Because she's telling me, tell Mum I'm strong enough to accept that I've gone. I feel there was an impact when she passed."

Jade confirms this.

"And I do see a road-side accident. But they're driving on the wrong side of the road, so I'm not really sure why..."

"She was in Greece."

"Okay, that explains it. I wasn't sure why they were on the wrong side of the road. She says it wasn't her fault, because the other ones were speeding. Do you understand? I feel maybe there was a bus or a coach in connection with this."

"A bus hit her car."

"That's why I'm seeing a bus. The name of Claire is given to me."

The woman starts crying. Now she can barely answer as she chokes out a reply. "My daughter."

"She tells me she is very much here with you, and she tells me, I love you so much, Mum. She absolutely adores you. She tells me you've been doing some writing. About her. She calls it 'Claire's mandates'."

Jade is so choked up she can't speak at all, she can only nod.

"She's telling me she's always around you, and she knows things haven't been that great for you since she passed. She says give my love to my sister, so I take it she's got a sister."

Jade nods.

"She says her sister is looking fantastic, although she's got a bit of a horrible boyfriend."

Jade nods vigorously.

"She tells me she's got a better-looking bloke up here. So Claire's got herself a boyfriend, too, up there in the spirit world. Has she been gone about seven years?"

"Ten."

"I see. It's a little hard for me to judge the timing because I'm only going by how she's dressed. She tells me that you were the best mum in the world. She tells me that she chose you out of all the mothers in the world, and that she's up there working with the angels. She's helping babies and young children when they cross over. Was she on holiday when she was killed?"

"She was."

"And she was just about to come back, wasn't she? That's what she's telling me."

The words come out of Jade as if they are being ripped from her throat: "In two days."

"She's telling me that the way you found out was absolutely despicable. And that no compassion was shown to you. She says she was sitting with you when you found out the news. Was she a bit of a daddy's girl?"

"No."

"Okay, well, she's talking about him and says he's gone a bit peculiar. I don't know what she means by that."

Through her tears, Jade laughs a little.

"I do feel she's very much here with you. Who has been feeling sick?"

"My daughter."

"Is she pregnant?"

"I hope not." says Jade. "She just had one."

"I think she's going to be pregnant again. Claire's telling me that her sister's going to be knocking them out like it's going out of fashion. I do feel that she's a lovely girl, your other daughter, and that there are some good things that will come her way soon. Claire says whatever life throws at you all, she's always there with you. You've also lost your dad, haven't you?"

Jade shakes her head.

"Then it's your husband's dad, because Claire says she's got Grandad there with her."

"Yes, my husband's father."

"And he's going on about his watch. Something about his watch. Someone has nicked his watch. He's very upset about that. Who is John?"

"My husband's brother."

"They are also telling me that there was a connection with... four birthdays in one month? Does that make sense?"

"We have a month like that."

"And also she says there was a birthday right around the time of her death."

"Yes, just before."

"Who used to call her 'Claire bear'?"

Jade's tears are flowing as she manages to say, "My husband."

"She says she loves you, and she's never far away from you, and the tingling feeling you get over your nose is her giving you a kiss. Do you understand this?"

Jade nods vigorously.

"And someone has been having trouble with their ears. I don't know if it's the baby, but I do feel someone on the earth plane is having trouble with their ears..."

"It's my mother-in-law."

"Thank you. Because Claire keeps telling me about this ear problem. But she says that it's only selective deafness."

Jade laughs at this.

"She's sending down her love, and she's telling me that the baby's perfect."

Jade doesn't respond.

"Is she? " Loraine asks. "How is the baby?"

"She's just fine."

"How old?"

"Seven months."

"Have you got three grandchildren?"

"No. My son's got one, four months old. So I have two grandchildren."

"There is another one that will be arriving soon," Loraine tells her. "You might end up being like the old woman who lived in a shoe if they keep carrying on. Who's Nicola?"

"I don't know."

"She's a friend of Claire's. Someone who has passed away and she's met with up there. Someone from way back. A friend from school. But she says 'Mum, Nicola's only just gone.' And I do feel she's met up with quite a few people. And with that she says God bless and thank you."

"Thank you," says Jade, then manages to add, "very much."

Although the session isn't over yet, Jade picks up her bag and is already making her way out of the back of the room, her hand across her cheeks that are puffy and red. As the double doors close behind her, the room goes quiet. I can't blame her for leaving. It is almost too emotional for me, and I've only been watching. The audience, myself included, seems to be equally stunned, as well as embarrassed at having witnessed the depths of such pain. I exchange a look with the woman sitting next to me. I don't know her, but I can read her expression. She, like myself, is shocked speechless by this reading that Loraine has pulled up out of nowhere. It is one thing to read the crossing of a grandparent, a parent, or even a spouse. But it is an entirely different kind of pain when a child dies too young, because this type of loss affects not only the heart, and the quality of the person's days, but it stomps along the entire length of a person's future, and perhaps even beyond.

Although she has already left, Jade's pain still colours the mood and drenches the room like a rain cloud.

Loraine takes a drink of water. "Is anyone bored?"

"No," erupts a woman near the front. "Are you?"

"Just freezing cold," Loraine says. She rolls up her sweater and shows her forearm. All up and down her skin, the fine hairs are standing so erect that I can see the effect from a dozen seats away.

"Good heavens!" gasps the woman in front.

"Exactly," says Loraine. "I'm not only clairaudient -- able to hear from the other side -- but I am also clairsensitive. This means I can feel what they feel. It comes so fast I don't always even know what I'm saying. You'll notice that sometimes I swear.

Particularly if the person swore in life. And I have to tell the audience, 'Don't get mad at me.' Because I don't have any control over what *they* want to say. Unfortunately, I hear it at the same time that I'm giving it. And sometimes, like just now, I feel like I've just put my foot in it, and I think, oh my God, what have I done this time? But I can't change it, because for me, that's the way it comes."

I don't envy Loraine that feeling. No one else seems to either, and the room is in serious need of levity.

Loraine provides it. "Did you know my daughter is here with us today? Stand up, Kayleigh."

KAYLEIGH

A pretty young girl seated near the back stands up, shyly.

"Kayleigh has the gift, as well," Loraine tells us. "Would you all like to see a demonstration?"

"Yes!" we reply, eager for anything that will shift this mood.

Loraine nods to her daughter. "Kayleigh, would you like to give us a reading?"

With the gentlest of self-conscious nods, Kayleigh agrees. Then she looks around at the room. It is a large crowd.

"No pressure," says Loraine, helpfully. "Right, everyone?"

Kayleigh rolls her eyes, not pleased that her mother has inadvertently revealed to us how nervous she is.

But, like a trooper, Kayleigh walks up and down the aisles, hesitant, until she finally stops beside a dark-haired woman. Once she is there, her hesitation is gone.

"Hello. What is your name?" Kayleigh asks.

"I'm Kelly."

"Hello, Kelly. Do you, by any chance, wear a piece of jewellery that belonged to someone named Corrine?"

The woman shakes her head no. Kayleigh is not daunted. "Then, was her name Kathleen?"

The woman is surprised. "Yes, she was my aunt. I have her pendant."

Kayleigh has found her stride and continues. "Did someone have problems with their back? I am seeing a problem there, particularly with the kidneys, and it was so severe that... did he die from this?"

"My father," the woman responds. "He died from kidney failure."

Kayleigh looks quietly relieved she got it right, twice in a row.

Loraine smiles. "Good, isn't she? She sings, too. Give her a round of applause, everyone."

The room responds, and Kayleigh goes back to her chair, glad to be out of the hot seat.

During the rest of the hour, Loraine reads eight more people. Some get short messages, some have extended readings. None of the rest are as emotional as Jade's reading, but the accuracy rate is just as high. Every person Loraine comes to seems pleased and a little astonished she has chosen them to talk to, and glad to hear messages that make perfect sense to them. In my rough estimate, based on the positive and negative replies, it seems that Loraine is running somewhere around an eighty percent accuracy rate. It's not one hundred percent but still it's inexplicably high. This, I discover, is about par for her shows. It would be easier to understand if she was making general comments that could apply across the board (you want to be in love, you like children, you have great-grandparents on the other side) but much of what Loraine says is not general. She delivers specific information, specific names, and the vast majority of what she says to a person would not apply to anyone else in the room.

At the end of the hour, I feel drained and exhausted. Just watching and recording the session makes me feel as though I've been on an emotional roller-coaster, the crazy-mad one that slams you into your harness as it spins and turns you against the force of gravity. I feel something equally potent here in this room, with these bonds of love that have crossed the great divide of death to deliver messages of continued support. It was amazing enough to experience it for myself when I had my private reading. But watching Loraine read several people, one after another in rapid fire, as if it is the easiest thing in the world, has compounded that feeling. At the end of her show, I feel like I need a break -- a few moments to process everything I've just seen.

But Loraine has no time to stop. She's booked solid with private readings for the rest of the day, so she must hurry downstairs to her booth to catch her next client, and the one after that, with an endless parade of twenty minute appointments, without a break, until the exhibition shuts down for the night at 6 p.m.

I wonder how she keeps up with the pace and the demands of staying on schedule. I know that in twenty years of going to my daughters' teacher appointments, with their carefully pre-arranged time slots, every single one of those parent evenings has run over. By the end of those school open house nights, the schedule is so ridiculously skewed that it throws the parents into a frenzy as they try to talk to each of their child's teachers despite the overruns that have bled into the next time slot.

But somehow, Loraine manages to keep her appointments on track, even though she's dealing with the complicated task of juggling the needs of the voices in this world, with the messages from elsewhere.

How does she manage it? How can she deal with both worlds at once and still maintain her sanity, her sense of time, and her sense of humour? How does one balance it all? It's a question worth asking, so I make note of it, and later, I get my chance.

Chapter 5

EMBRACING HER TALENT

Loraine's life has been less than idyllic. Her first husband, Pete, was a violent man. They met when she was just eighteen. She fell pregnant very soon, and she stayed with him until she was thirty-two.

Pete was an entertainer, and moved their growing family to Tenerife in the Canary Islands where he worked in the clubs. But while Loraine was at home caring for their five children, he was out getting into trouble with other women and drugs.

There was another significant man in Loraine's life. It was her spirit guide, Ramos. From a child she had sensed an Egyptian man around her, but she didn't know who he was until she was about fifteen, when he "introduced" himself to her as a spirit who had once lived in Egypt as a man named Ramos, during the days of the pharaohs. Sometimes she is visited by other spirit guides who also relay messages, including her great-grandmother. But Ramos is her main guide, because from the time he introduced himself, his presence has always been with her, acting as a bridge to bring her messages from others who have crossed over to the other side.

Ramos "told" Loraine that during his life on earth, he had worked as a scribe for one of the last of the great pharaohs, Ramses III. Loraine always assumed it was true but had no way to check it. Some years later, Loraine went on holiday to Egypt. One of the stops on the tour was a trip to Cairo with a visit to the Museum of Egypt. There was a section on Ramses III upstairs and Loraine was eager to explore the history of Ramses III and finally verify the identity of Ramos.

Unfortunately, the exhibit on Ramses III was closed for refurbishment and she wasn't allowed to go in. Disappointed, she got back into the mini-bus for the rest of the tour, which took the group to the town of Taba. There, the bus driver asked the passengers if he could pick up his friend along the way.

They agreed, and when the bus driver's friend got into the van, he turned out to be an Egyptologist who specialized in the history of the pharaohs. Loraine asked him if he knew anything about an ancient Egyptian named Ramos, and the scholar said that Ramos was the right hand man of Pharaoh Ramses III, and in fact, was so important that he was buried with the pharaoh by the Nile near the Valley of the Kings. The scholar didn't realize he was confirming something Loraine had felt since she was a teenager.

As Loraine explains it, she sees Ramos not as a solid being but instead a sort of mist. I have to admit, for a while I wasn't so convinced that Loraine's messages actually came from a spirit named Ramos. I knew her messages had startling accuracy, but I wasn't sure how it came to her or if she just somehow "knew". But I shed my doubts about Ramos when a member of her audience saw him, too, and described him to me just as Loraine describes him.

At the time that Loraine's marriage to Pete was falling apart, Ramos "told" her to leave the marriage and Tenerife. She wasn't working at the time, and had very little money except what she had saved for the kids. She wondered how she could possibly support them all, a mother with five children and no job. Her spirit guide advised her that her gift would be enough to see her through.

Finally, she agreed. It was 1995 when she pooled all her resources and bought one-way tickets back to England for herself and the children: Cheryl (born in 1984), Daniel (1986), Kayleigh (1991), Emmaleigh (1993), and baby Billy, less than a year old. With nothing to her name but what she could carry, she arrived back in England with her children, and moved into her parents' house.

Loraine wondered how she could possibly support herself and her children. Having married at eighteen and immediately started her family, she didn't have any particular job skills or training. But then she saw an announcement in a newspaper for a psychic show. She called on a Tuesday, and by the Thursday, she found herself at the show, with her own booth, conducting readings. She had no agent, no manager, just two chairs, a small folding table, and her gift – that rare ability to connect, through Ramos and her other spirit guides, to souls on the other side.

At that first psychic fair, a few people trickled in. Then they told their friends, who told their friends, and before she knew it, she was booked with readings every single day. Ever since then, her client base has been very steady, and on a typical week, she might do up to two hundred readings over the seven days.

At times she has been called upon by law enforcement officials to help with difficult cases. One crime involved two girls who had been murdered. When the police investigation stalled, the authorities contacted a number of psychics, including Loraine. She was the one who told them she felt there was a school connection involved. Sure enough, the murderer turned out to be a man employed by the local school who had been stalking the girls, and he was apprehended. [Author's note: Although this was a very well-known case, Loraine prefers not to give additional details as she does not wish to further her career or reputation based on the tragedy of others. Another person was in the room with her when she gave the information to the police, and this individual has since made public claims in the media as being responsible for solving the case. In the interviews, this individual has not mentioned that the information actually came from Loraine.]

Loraine has seen other mediums work, some real, some fake, and can spot a phoney right away. As she explains it, the fakes don't have a spirit guide hovering around, giving them answers. Now that she is attuned to seeing Ramos, she can see other people's spirit guides as well.

After she began giving private readings, she met Darren, her second husband, who was eight years younger. He was a kind man, and in 1998, they had a child together, Amelia, to cement their bond. But with him being so much younger, he had a hard time dealing with her tribe of children. When the older ones became teenagers, it became more than he could handle.

In 2008, Loraine lost her mother, Maureen, to a cerebral haemorrhage. Maureen was only sixty-six and went very fast. Loraine knew that her mother would be all right in the spirit world, and has "seen" her mother since, at times of crisis. For instance, when Loraine later had the miscarriage, her mother appeared to her, beside the tiny little boy's spirit.

Still, losing Maureen's comforting presence in her daily life was very hard on Loraine.

To cheer her up, Loraine's daughter Emmaleigh signed her up for a chat line. There Loraine met Mark, who was in the process of extricating himself from a difficult relationship. Soon after Loraine met him, they discovered that he had signed up for the chat line on the same hour that Loraine joined it. Three months after they started dating, he proposed, and they eloped for a whirl-wind honeymoon to Scotland.

I find it surprising that Loraine has been married so many times. It seems amazing that she can deliver so many useful messages to others, while managing to get things wrong for herself. She explains that this is normal for mediums. While she receives messages for other people, she rarely gets any hints about her own life. Nine times out of ten, she says she has no idea what's coming. If she did, she could have avoided a lot of problems.

She feels that if she were in serious danger, she would get a warning. But, as she explains, sometimes Ramos will "tell" her to be careful, but she doesn't always listen. Just getting a message, even if it is from your dead Egyptian spirit guide, doesn't mean you have to pay attention, and she enjoys the freedom of making her own mistakes. Although she'll be the first to tell you that she has made more than her fair share.

Chapter 6

THE CAMBRIDGE SHOW
March 2010

In March of 2010, Loraine contacts me. Her schedule has eased up a bit and she's got some time to get rolling on the book again. She has scheduled four shows this month and I agree to attend them all -- my very own Loraine Rees medium marathon.

The first is up in Cambridge. Unlike the previous shows I've attended, affiliated with a big weekend exhibition, the Cambridge event is a stand-alone show called "An Evening of Clairvoyance with Loraine Rees." Unconstrained by the format of a larger organization, this show will last three hours. Coming from south of London, I expect it to take three hours to get there, so I give myself an extra hour, just to be safe. But I have seriously underestimated the traffic and it takes me over five hours before I make it there. By the time I arrive upstairs in the meeting room of a large, glitsy David Lloyd Centre, I have missed the first half of the show. It is intermission time as I settle in, ready to catch the last ninety minutes.

THE THREE WITCHES

After the intermission, Loraine walks up and down the aisles, then comes to a row where three women sit together. This time, she is not speaking to a single individual, she is talking to the group.

"Who has lost their husband?" Loraine asks. "Who just passed?"

"That was Uncle Ray," replies one of the women.

"I feel that someone had cancer," Loraine says.

"Ray," the second one says with a nod.

"He's telling me that he always had something to say, and he didn't like being trumped. He says the witches never let him get a word in. He's calling you witches?"

The women find this hilarious.

"I'm getting that there was a big family argument. It's been going on about five years. Do you understand? And someone has been very two-faced."

They nod in agreement. It is all pleasant and jovial until Loraine adds, "And someone was murdered. There's been lots of covering up, especially in the past eighteen months, but two people knew what went on."

The women are quiet now, eager to hear more.

Loraine continues. "It's like I can't get to the bottom of it because people are burying their heads under water over it, do you understand?"

More solemn confirmation.

"And who wants to drown the bastard who did it?"

"We all want that," says the first woman in the row.

"There's two people involved," Loraine reaffirms. "Not just one. There's two people who knew what went on. And I do feel there was a lot of... who's Stevie?"

"Oh, my God, yes!" gasps the second woman.

"And somebody called Dennis? Already passed."

"He was my husband."

"He just wants to validate that he's still around you. And someone is called Tony. And also something to do with a memorial. Was it three weeks ago? Or was it three months?"

"The memorial was three months ago."

"I do feel there's another court date coming up," Loraine says. "And there will be a lot of digging to try to find out what happened. Now, who is Ian?"

The women look at each other, but the name doesn't seem to ring any bells.

"Ian?" Loraine says. "Or Elaine? It starts with a strong E sound."

For a moment, none of them can validate who this might be. Then one of them says, "Aunt Enid?"

"No, no," Loraine tells her. "Enid's all right. She's not involved in the murder mystery. No, Enid's a good girl. And someone hung himself. He wants to say he's sorry, because he didn't realize all the shit it would cause."

The women nod glumly.

"And somebody likes to... what's this? Someone likes to have their toes sucked?"

All three women explode with laughter. The whole room roars. This is followed by a great amount of good-natured ribbing and toe-sucking denial. The third woman in the row, who has been the quietest of the trio so far, makes the loudest protest, which has everyone in stitches. It makes me wonder if there's something to this toe-sucking rumour after all.

Not that it matters. The fact is that Loraine has exposed this family's dark vein of murder and suicide, to a room full of people from their own home-town, and has managed to leave these women with tears of mirth and delight on their cheeks. Whether one believes in clairvoyance or not, Loraine's ability to work a room is a real *tour de force*.

EMMA

Loraine approaches a girl with long hair in the second row, late teens or early twenties, who identifies herself as Emma.

"I'm seeing two men," Loraine tells her. "One is your father. He says you didn't speak to him for a long time. He says, 'she fecking hated me.' Is that true? That you hated your father?"

Emma squirms uncomfortably in her seat, with the slightest of nods.

"I'm sorry that it's true," says Loraine. "He says he wished he had been more of a man when he was alive. He passed when he was quite young, and you didn't really know who he was. Who told you he was dead? Who told you he was gone?"

"My grandad."

"And he's just passed?"

"Yes."

"Sorry, Em. But your father tells me he does love you. Your father tells me that you're a good girl, nothing like your mother."

This elicits a nervous laugh from the crowd.

Loraine continues. "I'm going to say he's still around you, whether you like it or not. I'm seeing flowers and baby's breath. It's a funeral. He says you put something on his grave after he died."

"I put a balloon on it."

"He saw that, and he appreciated it. He says he really didn't have anything to do with the family when he was alive. But he's telling me that you have two things from him, two items that were his, and he wants you to cherish them. I feel he was very selfish. A selfish git [a person with no manners]. Not an old git, he was a young git, because he died before he got old. Who is Paul?"

"My uncle."

"Your father is very jealous of your relation with Paul. He says he was your dad, and should have acted like it but he was so young that he just couldn't be a dad to anyone. He tells me he was very sick when he died. He says he was in his death-bed for four days. Does that make any sense?"

"It was four days after he died that they found him."

"He says the maggots were eating his eyeballs. He says he could look down and see that. It wasn't very nice. He says nobody really knew him. Who was the alcoholic?"

"He was."

"I feel that the reason he died was that he fell down the stairs and hit his head. And who is Peter, because he died from alcohol as well."

Emma isn't sure who Peter might be.

"Well, your father wishes he had the balls to be a better man when he was alive. He says he was too busy thinking about himself. He tells me there was a birthday right around his passing."

"Mine."

"And he didn't get you anything. Did you see him only twice? Why is he telling me you only saw him twice?"

"I only saw him two times. When I was very young."

"He is telling me you were sick over him, but things were so up and down with him and your mum, that he just couldn't be around. And with that he sends his love."

The room applauds and Loraine starts to walk away. But then she walks back to Emma.

"Who is Michael?" Loraine asks. "Because just now as I walked away, I could hear your father calling for Michael."

"Michael is my brother."

"But Michael is still here on the earth plane, right?"

Emma agrees.

"What's wrong with Michael? I do feel like he's got a lot of growing up to do."

Emma nods at that.

"And who's been smoking the marijuana?"

"Michael."

"Is that all? How about you?"

Emma smiles, preferring not to answer that one.

"Your father is crying, and he's very sad that he has to say these things to you now, and not when he was alive and should have. And... he's telling me that someone had to crash into his house to remove his body."

Emma confirms that they had to break in to get him.

"He tells me he was in an awful state, going kind of black. And he wasn't in bed, he was just sitting there. He said he had a remote control on one side and a beer on the other."

"Yes."

"He says he's really sorry, and with that I'll say God bless."

Loraine reads eight more people, and nearly everything is readily confirmed. From my estimate, based on the responses, her accuracy rate at this show is running particularly high, even for her.

Ninety minutes later, when the show is over, I catch up with Emma. She tells me she is still in shock.

"It was so personal," Emma says. "There were things about my father that nobody knew, like the two items I kept. No one knew about that but me. Or the number of times I saw him in my life."

Emma can't get over that Loraine knew how her father was found, sitting dead in his easy chair, with the TV remote in one hand and a can of beer in the other. She's right; it is not something you could just guess. I can't get over it either, or clear the image from my mind. What a shattering thing, for that image to be this girl's remembrance and legacy of her father.

Emma says that everyone calls her brother Woody. Few people use or even know that his given name is Michael. Her father, of course, had known.

Emma tells me that after her reading, she slipped out of the room and called her mother, to ask if she remembered someone named Peter. It was the only thing from the reading that didn't make sense. On the phone, her mother explained that Peter was a friend of her father's from a long time ago. An alcoholic friend. Her mother isn't sure if Peter has passed away or not, because she lost contact with him a long time ago.

Emma is pleased to have had these messages and this positive closure with her father. She is more than pleased, she is positively beaming. There is a light in this young woman's face that wasn't there before. With his lifetime of regrets and failures, these few words delivered through Loraine are the sum total of all the love she has ever received from her father. But it is more than she ever expected. More than she dreamed was possible from him.

For her, it is enough.

And although it has been ninety minutes since her reading when I finally get to talk to her, and snap a quick photo of her with Loraine, this young woman, so long denied a father's love, is still shining with an inner glow.

DEAN

As I pack up my notes and my tape recorder to leave, I notice a group of four friends, two men and two women, who have stayed late to talk to me. I have not met them before, and I wasn't here when they got their readings, but they are still here after nearly everyone else has gone home because they feel it's important to tell me their story.

Stuart, supported by his friends Darren, Natalie, and Sarah, explains that his nephew Dean was killed a while ago during difficult circumstances. While Stuart was struggling to deal not only with his grief but also the terrible injustice of the situation, he went to one of Loraine's shows. He was curious although he didn't expect much. To his surprise, his nephew came through, via Loraine, and detailed the circumstances of his death. Stuart already knew how Dean had died, so what Loraine said did not tell him anything new. However, it provided hard-to-ignore validation that it really was Dean's presence that was coming through. Then, through Loraine, Dean pleaded with Stuart not to make things worse, and to refrain from taking matters into his own hands.

Stuart was moved to make a promise to his departed nephew that he wouldn't take action and do anything rash. It wasn't easy, letting it go, but over time he has realized it was the right path. Two wrongs do not make a right, and it has put his mind to rest knowing he is doing what Dean would want.

Natalie concurs. She says she originally came to Loraine's show to be entertained. But after that first time, this entire group of friends has returned to hear from Dean. And at every one of Loraine's shows they have attended, Dean has come through for them. They were not believers before, but ever since that first "Evening of Clairvoyance," whenever Loraine comes to town, there is nowhere else they plan to be but in her audience, ready and hoping to reconnect once again, no matter how briefly, to this remarkable soul with his message of forgiveness and peace.

PHOTO GALLERY

Loraine's mother, Maureen, as a child. Maureen had psychic talent as well, but chose not to develop it.

Maureen (left) with a young Loraine about thirteen years old. At this point, Loraine knew she was clairvoyant but didn't share that with her friends.

Loraine didn't explore her talent professionally until she found herself the sole support of five children. Loraine (left) with two of her children, Cheryl and Billy.

Three more daughters: Kayleigh, Amelia, and Emmaleigh. Of all her children, Kayleigh (left) has shown the most psychic talent so far and occasionally joins Loraine in her shows

John from the West Sussex Show with his wife, Joyce. He received a message from his uncle who had left him a special letter when he went to war.

Loraine (left) with Emma who was pleased to hear from her father, a man who was found in unusual circumstances.

In memory of Dean: Four friends come together to reconnect with a forgiving soul.

Loraine addresses the audience at her show at the Mind Body Spirit Exhibition at Kempton Park Racecourse, March 201

After Penny lost her daughter, she has often felt a gentle tug on her ear.
How did Loraine know?

Diane got a short message of four special names. "What more do I
need?"

Jenny was "elated" so many of her relatives came through. She was always "daddy's girl."

Susan wasn't sure at first if she wanted her ex-husband to come through, but when she decided it would be okay, he did.

Lorna didn't understand the American connection until Loraine asked about war-time romance with American soldiers. Then Lorna's face turned nearly as red as her jacket.

Sally is once again a proud mother. Now, even death can not take that from her.

Jack, his future mother-in-law Mandy, and Della. Jack missed a football match to come to Loraine's show, while Mandy won a door prize.

Jen was delighted the white feather showed up at a strategic moment in the show. Her auntie Diana had promised before she died to bring her a white feather if she could.

Three generations: Loraine with her father Henry (left) and son Billy (right).

The Brentwood demonstration room   starts to fill up before Loraine arrives. My friend Sue Bohane prepares to record the show on video. Sue was supportive of the project but initially sceptical until Loraine told her, "Your mother says to take the horns by the bull." Apparently, this had been Sue's mother's unique twist on the saying.

Paula and Chris from the Brentwood Show. Loraine knew Paula worked near Big Ben. Afterwards, Paula showed me a photo on her mobile phone with a view of Big Ben from her office.

Wendy, Margaret, and Jane from the Brentwood Show. While Wendy and Margaret received readings and Jane did not, she still felt "well-entertained."

People leave Loraine's Brentwood Show with a lift in their step.

Janice and Joan with Loraine at her booth at the Linton Show. Joan had specifically "asked" her husband to come through and tell her he had the boy with him, and he did. Janice's messages about butterflies had special meaning for her.

Pauline and her daughter Sue got readings at the Brentwood and the Linton Shows. Through Loraine, Pauline's husband "gave" her two messages: that there is indeed a God, and her cooking skills need help.

Beverly was startled to see the misty form of Loraine's spirit guide shoot past her.

Contemplating it all after the Kempton Park Show. It can be a lot to take in.

Intermission at the Peterborough Show.

These women got readings. Their expressions show how they felt about the messages they received.

Loraine with Hisham, a neurosurgeon who was surprised to receive validation from his father. Hisham's father, who risked his life to save freedom fighters during the French occupancy of Syria, died in 1969.

Passing on the gift? Loraine with her first grandchild, baby Ayla.

The room where Loraine conducted private readings and the lights put on spontaneous flashing displays. The light switch is on the wall near the corner; no dimmer switch here.

An artist's sketch of Ramos, Loraine's main spirit guide, who had "told" Loraine he had been the scribe to Pharaoh Ramses III. Years later on a trip to Egypt, a scholar confirmed that Pharaoh Ramses III ruled with the help of his right hand man, who was named Ramos.

According to Loraine, Ramos liked this sketch so much that he suggested it for the front cover of the book. It makes perfect sense that any spirit guide of Loraine's would have a big personality.

Chapter 7

THE KEMPTON PARK EXHIBITION

March 2010

A week later, I arrive at the second show of my Loraine Rees marathon. This time her show will only be an hour long, as it is part of the Mind Body Soul Exhibition at the Kempton Park Racecourse. As she often does, Loraine begins the show by asking the audience members to uncross their legs. As she explains, crossing the legs can block the solar plexus and block messages.

Someone asks her what is it like to be able to communicate with spirits. Loraine says it doesn't feel strange or weird, she just feels it is something we all have inside of us, to various degrees. She equates the ability to riding a bike, with different people having different techniques for accomplishing the task. The way she sees it, some people leave their bikes when they're done with school, but she's still pedalling away.

TRUDY

Loraine approaches a woman named Trudy and asks if she remembers her grandmother. Trudy does. Loraine feels that Trudy is a lot like her grandmother, as they both tend to be thinkers. Loraine asks if Grandma was "moany" and Trudy tells us that Grandma complained a lot. Loraine says, "Grandma is saying the same thing about you."

Loraine also senses a "dad" link on the other side, and Trudy confirms that her father has crossed. Loraine says he was the sort of person who started talking about one thing, then switched to another. She says Trudy's father was always two conversations behind, and then asks Trudy who had throat or lung cancer.

Trudy confirms it was her father who died this way. Loraine says he had to have oxygen near the end, and that sometimes when Trudy notices the smell of oxygen around her, it is her father drawing close. Loraine claims that the robin Trudy saw the other day was him, and asks that the next time she sees the robin, would she please feed it, because her father was always hungry.

Trudy agrees, that he had a big appetite, and was indeed on oxygen at the end.

Loraine continues. "One of your aunties used to read the tea leaves. She thought she was a bit of a gypsy. She says you could do that as a child as well. Who went off to Canada?"

"My husband," Trudy says. "But he's not dead."

Loraine smiles. "He doesn't have to be dead to go to Canada. I feel you're going to be seeing him again. Just watch that space."

Trudy doesn't seem pleased.

"Oh, yes," Loraine insists. "He's going to be looking for you. You haven't seen him for years, have you? You wouldn't piss on him if he was on fire, would you?"

Trudy laughs, but she also agrees.

Loraine tells her, "He's going to try to get back into your life. Who is David?"

Trudy explains it is her partner.

"Good!" Loraine says. "I want to say, don't roll over David, because the ex might be trying to get back into the bed. Your dad and all of them up there are laughing their heads off about that." We are all laughing our heads off down here, as well. Even Trudy.

A KIND FACILITATOR

Loraine continues with Trudy's reading. "I do feel that David has had a sadness lately. Has he recently lost someone close?"

"Yes, his father."

"He doesn't cope well with the sadness, does he?" Loraine turns to the row of people beyond Trudy. "Wait... who is Bob? Or Robert? Down this row? He's very insistent."

A woman down the row says she knows a Robert.

Loraine asks if she knows two Roberts in the spirit world, a big Robert and a little Robert. And if big Robert had been the kind of person who always interrupted.

The woman says Robert was her brother, and no, he wasn't rude or pushy.

Loraine looks beyond the woman and asks who killed himself? Who hung himself?

Another woman in the row responds. "Oh, God yes, my nephew hung himself recently."

"I'm so sorry," Loraine tells her. "He's saying he's sorry, too, and he wants you to tell his mother that. He's telling me he wasn't found right away and it was his second attempt. There were two birthdays near the time of his death, and he says someone put lots of roses down for him. He says she puts red and white roses out for him for some reason."

"His mother does that. Red and white."

"He tells me he went through a hard time. He says the last four years of his life were a battle, and he says he was in a little trouble with the law. Did you know that?"

"No."

"He says there were a lot of things he took to his grave with him. He's really crying up there. He tells he was a little shy about coming through but... he says there were three nice things read about him at his memorial."

"Yes, his mum and his sister read something."

"And his other sister read something, too? I'm seeing three things being read. Who is Mark? Or Martin?"

The woman doesn't know.

"You might have to look back for that," Loraine says. "It was a friend who also took his life. I do feel that your nephew was a really nice guy, and he tells me that now he's all right."

Loraine goes back to Robert's sister. "I'm hearing from Robert again. He had a lovely smile, didn't he? He tells me someone was writing a letter to him."

The woman can't confirm that.

"Then hold on to it," Loraine tells her, "because he's quite insistent about it."

Loraine turns to the woman next to her.

"Are you connected to her?"

This other woman nods her head.

"I want to say that your female friend that passed, the one who was very young, about nineteen, is here."

The woman confirms she had a good friend when she was in her early twenties who passed too soon.

Loraine continues. "She tells me she saw you right before her death, and she tried to tell you she had problems, but she just couldn't get the words out. Don't blame yourself. She tells me she

"She tells me she was really muddled up. She says she was pregnant at the time of her death, did you know that? "

This is news to the woman.

"It's true, because she's got the baby with her. Who did cocaine? Why is she showing me coke?"

The woman doesn't have a clue about who it could be.

"Who was she seeing at the time of her death?" Loraine asks.

"Oh," says the woman, with obvious disdain.

Loraine says, "I do feel she went down a different line of friendship. She tells me the last five years, you didn't really know a lot of what went on in her life. She tells me she's fine now, and she's really glad you came here. It was Robert who brought her in. He brought through the nephew, too. His sister's right, he's not pushy. He's just been bringing everyone through. He's watching after all the souls today, especially the ones who were young and busty, like your friend. He really likes them."

Loraine turns back to Robert's sister, who is giggling at that. "It seems your brother was a bit of a perv, wasn't he?"

The sister shrugs.

"Yes, he was," Loraine insists with a smile. "I quite like him." This gets a chuckle.

Then she returns her attention to the woman with the female friend who died young. "I do feel your friend is fine now. Someone sang her favourite song at her funeral. And she wants you to know she's okay. She says she's got a bloke up there."

Loraine turns back to the sister. "Maybe it's your brother, Robert, the old perv. Oh, he thinks that's funny, and they're all having a good laugh up there."

That wouldn't surprise me. I know we are having a good laugh down here.

"And did your father pass?" she asks the same woman.

The woman shakes her head.

"Then your grandfather? I am seeing a man with a trilby."

"Grandad."

"I'm seeing problems with the stomach," Loraine says.

"Cancer of the tummy region, do you understand that?"

"Yes, my aunt."

"She's quite feisty, wasn't she. And who plays the piano?"

The woman shakes her head, unable to come up with a piano player.

"No one plays the piano?" Loraine asks, not willing to give up. "Really? How about the keyboards?"

"Oh!" The woman seems surprised. "I do that."

"They're telling me you're excellent, and you should play more. And not just for the boys. Your grandad loves to hear you play. Even though he's tone deaf. And with that I'll say God bless."

I can barely keep up with the way Loraine has bounced around the row, delivering messages to one person, then the next. This is what John Edward calls a "me, too" event, when the readings bounce around the room as different spirits add their "voice" to the discussion. It is exhausting to watch. I can't imagine what it would be like to orchestrate it.

Then Loraine walks down the middle aisle of the room, and sees a woman she recognizes. "You were here last year," she says. "When your mother came through."

"Right," says the woman.

Loraine asks the room, "Was anyone else here for that? Does anyone remember that?"

A few people scattered around the room nod in agreement.

I am thinking Loraine must have a very good memory, to recall specific people who received messages. With up to two hundred private readings a week and all her shows, that is an awful lot of faces. Either Loraine's memory is phenomenal, or that reading was.

Loraine explains. "A year ago, right here in this room, her mother came through, and was so angry we could all feel it."

"That's right," says the woman.

Loraine explains to the rest of us. "The windows got dark, the walls were shaking, doors rattling. I was so scared I almost shit myself."

A few people giggle, but her remark can't fully gloss over the serious edge. This is the first time I have heard Loraine talk about dark and tangible consequences during a reading. She has mentioned lights and radios turning off and on, but never windows rattling and doors shaking. Loraine tells me later that she has done several readings for this woman throughout the past year, and fortunately with each reading, the mother's spirit gradually became calmer until the anger finally dissolved.

PENNY

Loraine approaches a woman who identifies herself as Penny.

"Have you lost a daughter?" Loraine asks. "I've got a daughter here. A baby girl, and she calls you Mum. Did you lose a baby?"

"Yes."

"It was a long time ago, because I do feel she's very grown up now. So I feel it was years ago that it happened. She just wants to validate that she's around you. And sometimes you feel a little tugging on your ear, and she tells me that it is her coming close to you. Now, you've lost your dad as well, haven't you, because I do feel there's a dad figure up there, and he's coming through quite strongly. He says there are things we find out up here we didn't know about in life. He says he loves his family very much. Very stiff upper lip. Very Victorian in his outlook on life. He says he's met up with his maker more than once. I've got your nan here, too. She had long hair and she liked to wear it up in a knot. She had lovely hair when she was a younger woman. There is also going to be someone in a hospital bed on the Earth. I'm smelling anaesthetic so just hold on to this, but I'm not seeing a funeral. They're all around you, your dad and your grannie, and sending their love. Your father says he's sorry he needed to get your attention by showing me the little girl standing there, but he really wanted to come through and say hello. They all love you very much. Did you know your mother lost one as well?"

Penny nods yes.

"And who's been sick? Acid indigestion or heart burn?"

Penny doesn't know.

"Just hold on to that, and with that I'll say goodbye and God bless."

QUESTIONS

Loraine reiterates that she feels everyone has a bit of sixth sense in them. She's just been able to develop hers to a greater extent. She says she's really quite normal, and insists that outside of work, she's really boring. Her uncle is in the audience today, and she asks him to confirm. With gentle grace, he declines to respond.

Loraine opens the session for a questioning period. A woman near the front asks where is the best place to try to develop her talent. She's been trying at home, but isn't too pleased with her progress.

Loraine advises that while you can practice at home, your own house might not necessarily be the best place because of all the distractions. She suggests that working in a group is best, because it is easier to concentrate when there are other people around doing the same thing. You might not be as tempted to pop off for a nice cup of tea.

According to Loraine, developing one's talent also depends on what the person wants to do with it. If the goal is to be a church medium, you could go to a spiritualist's church. If you wanted to be a stage medium, you would need to learn from someone who gets the messages fast. There are plenty of teachers you can find on the internet, and she feels it is important to find someone you gel with. If you don't have a good feeling about it, then that teacher is really not for you.

Loraine insists that everyone is born with psychic abilities, but when children start to go to school, they begin to focus on other things and often grow away from it.

Someone asks Loraine about death. Loraine feels quite strongly that when you die, you are not "gone," but have transferred over to the other side.

To illustrate this, Loraine relates an anecdote, based on her relationship with her spirit guide, Ramos. It happened while she was in the hospital under aesthetic for an operation. When she finally woke up, her surgeon said, "I didn't know you could speak Arabic."

Loraine didn't know either. In fact, she doesn't know a single word of the language. She didn't even realize that her spirit guide, Ramos, would have spoken Arabic, and not "Egyptian." However, her surgeon told her that while she was out, she was talking and mumbling in perfect Arabic.

Loraine doesn't remember any of that. What she does remember from the time she was under the surgeon's knife are glimpses of meeting up with her departed mother and grandmother. They told her not to worry about the operation because it would turn out fine. And it did.

A woman on the far left side of the room asks what she should do if she is working with psychic issues and starts to feel afraid. In situations like that, Loraine advises to ask for protection. This, she believes, is the job of a person's spirit guide, and what guides are meant to provide.

Loraine says her best advice is something that the spirits have told her over and over, a universal truth that applies to everyone. According to Loraine, you should trust your first thought. A person's initial and instinctive response, she claims, comes from the spirit world, from the person's guides who are charged with protecting each of us. According to Loraine, the first instinct is the right decision, the right choice. In contrast, a person's second thought on a question comes from his own mind, and it may lead him astray. In other words, given a choice between trusting your instincts and your thoughts, Loraine advises to follow your instinct.

Before the hour is up, Loraine walks up to a woman who identifies herself as Diane.

"I'm almost out of time," Loraine tells her, "but I want to give you a name. Bill."

Diane nods.

Loraine adds, "And James. Betty. And Lill, or Lillian. My goodness, Bill's met up with everyone up there."
It is a happy note to end on, and Diane smiles, looking quietly pleased.

Outside in the hall after the session is over, I catch up with Trudy who tells me she was glad her father came through because they were very close. He was a big man, she explains, so of course he had a healthy appetite. She didn't know a great deal about her dad's mother who died quite young. And frankly, she is surprised her tea-leaf-reading auntie came through for her, because Trudy admits to being a spirited and naughty child, and she never thought her auntie liked her very much.

Then I talk to Penny, who lost a baby girl years ago, and often feels a slight tugging on her ear. Penny has seen a number of mediums and thinks that Loraine, while "unconventional and a bit of a character," is one of the best. She would rate Loraine's accuracy at eighty percent. However, some of the events Loraine has suggested happened before Penny's time, so for those, she can't confirm or deny them.

I thank Penny for taking the time to talk to me and I look around for the woman whose mother rattled the windows at Loraine's last Kempton Park show. I would really like to get her description of what happened, but she's already left.

By this time, most people have left except for one last person who has been patiently waiting to talk to me.

DIANE

The woman who has waited to see me is Diane. I flip through my notes and see that Diane received the last reading of the hour. It was almost an after-thought, and the shortest reading of all, not more than a few seconds. It was so quick I almost didn't bother to write it down. But here was Diane, who had waited very patiently to talk to me, after everyone else had gone off. I am happy to talk to her, but not entirely sure why she wants to.

"What did you think of your reading?" I ask.

Diane smiles. "It was extraordinary. I feel wonderful. Very relaxed. More than that, I feel like a great weight has been taken off of me. A weight I didn't even realize was there until it left."

I don't understand her reaction. Diane got nearly the shortest reading possible. In fact, it was just four names.

"It wasn't a very long reading," I say, trying to hide my confusion. But there is nothing confusing about Diane's reaction. The reading, as short as it was, has clearly proved very meaningful to her.

I ask, "What did you find that was so extraordinary about it?"

"Bill was my husband," says Diane. "The other names she gave were the names of my father, my mother, and my step-mother, the closest people to me, now gone. But now I know that they're not really gone. What more do I need?"

What more, indeed. Despite everything I have seen watching Loraine at work, the astonishing details, and the outrageous reveals, Diane's assessment of her very brief reading rivets me. I am in awe of the process, of Diane's transformation and inner peace, and this incredible gift that Loraine so willingly shares, as easily as breathing, and I am humbled all over again.

*Chapter **8***

PETERBOROUGH
March 2010

I've driven up north to a small town on the outskirts of Peterborough to attend Loraine's next show. This will be a long evening event, at least three hours, and Loraine lives near this town so I am expecting a lively crowd. The venue is a small sports centre with a soccer field out back. Every chair in the hall has been lined up facing forward to prepare for the show. The chairs fill up fast, with probably one hundred and fifty people who have paid to attend.

As the show starts, Loraine asks if anyone has seen her show before. Several people respond. I am wondering how many of these people are neighbours who have heard about her work and are curious to see what she does.

Loraine introduces me and invites people to talk to me during the break and after the show if they want to share their experiences for the book project. She announces that she will be taking questions later, and people can write them down and put them in the hat for her to pick out and answer later in the show. She also tells the audience they can contact her through her web site if they are interested in the development circle she plans to run, to help those wishing to develop their own psychic talent.

JENNY

Loraine approaches a woman named Jenny. She reads that Jenny's father, who has crossed over, is here. She senses a birthday has just passed. Jenny starts to say when her birthday is, but Loraine tells her, "Not your birthday. It's his!" Jenny relates her father's birthday was last month, in February.

Loraine mentions lung or throat cancer. Jenny seems confused. Loraine asks if it was her grandmother who had that. "Oh, yes!" says Jenny.

Loraine asks who Elsie was, and Jenny says it was her other grandmother. Loraine asks about the black dog who had the toilet-training problem, and tells Jenny the dog is up there with Grandma.

I have seen Loraine pick up on family pets before, mostly dogs and sometimes a favourite cat. One time an uncle came through and claimed his horse was up there with him. He had run a carriage business, and the faithful, dependable horse had been a big part of keeping the business going.

Loraine "gets" that someone Jenny knew had a scooter and used to attract girls on his scooter. She asks about Charlie and Bill, who also turn out to be relatives that have crossed.

Later, Jenny tells me she is "elated" to have heard from so many relatives. Usually it is just her father who comes through, but tonight she received greetings from so many others. She says she always comes to Loraine's shows when she can, because it is her chance to hear, once again, from her father. And as she explains, she was always "daddy's girl."

SUSAN

After Jenny's reading, Loraine crosses the room and heads towards me. I am hoping she doesn't read me right now. I've driven a long way to come up here and document this show, and Loraine talks so fast that it is all I can do to keep up with my notes and tapes and photos and get it all down. I am relieved when she stops before the woman sitting next to me on my right, who identifies herself as Susan.

Loraine asks Susan if she knows a Terry, alive, who has lost his dad. Susan says yes. Loraine tells her this dad would like people to visit his grave more often.

Then Loraine asks if David is Susan's husband. Again, Susan says yes. Loraine feels that David dreamt of his departed uncle and when Susan says it is true, Loraine tells Susan it was more than a dream, it was a visit.

Then Loraine says that she's got Big Grandad and Little Grandad with her, and also Susan's mum, who appreciated Susan talking about her the other day. Loraine asks who Jean or Joan is, and Susan explains that Joan is her mum's mother. Loraine asks if she's just passed because she feels Joan still walks around on the Earth. Susan explains that Joan passed within the last two years.

Loraine tells her that Mum's toe isn't black any more, and Susan is pleased to hear this. Then Loraine says she's hearing from Susan's first love, who has taken secrets to the grave with him, and asks Susan who had the difficult divorce. Susan admits there was a divorce in the family, but she doesn't want to talk about it.

Loraine senses that Susan has attended a lot of funerals lately, so many that Susan feels like the funeral queen. Susan agrees. Loraine "sees" a flower arrangement with nine roses. Loraine insists, "Not ten roses or a dozen, but nine."

Then Loraine tells Susan that her mother has met up with Elvis Presley, and even got a kiss. What a concept. I'm not sure Susan believes it. I'm not sure I believe it, but it's a fun way to wrap up the reading. As I look around, it seems to me that half the audience is day-dreaming about who they'd like to meet up with on the other side.

Next, Loraine approaches a woman named Eve. She asks if Eve is pregnant but Eve denies it. Loraine asks if she's sure, and again, Eve is adamant that she is not pregnant. Loraine tells her she better get on the job tonight because a baby is coming.

Loraine says Eve's nan is telling her that Eve will have two babies, one of each sex, by the same man. Eve can't confirm or deny any of this and seems confused by it all.

Loraine asks Eve if she's sure she doesn't want a baby. Eve explains that actually, she does.

"Good," Loraine says. "Then what are you doing here? You should be home making it."

JUDY

Loraine goes further down the row and asks, "Who died on a motorbike? Does anyone know someone who died on a motorbike?"

A woman named Judy responds. Loraine asks if it was her brother. Judy validates that it was. Loraine says she feels that he had a head or neck injury, and that it was an instant death. Judy explains that his neck snapped. Loraine says he's quite angry about being dead, and someone was crying at Christmas, and he stood with her. Was it Mum? Is Mum still alive? Judy says that Mum is still alive.

Loraine asks if her mum has a kettle that turns off and on, all by itself. Judy isn't sure. Loraine suggests that she ask her about it, and explains to us all that spirits like playing with electric appliances. Loraine says that spirits are made up of energy, so they can turn electrical things off and on, like television sets, and maybe even start watching naughty films if they want.

It's a silly concept and people enjoy the joke. But this isn't the first time Loraine has talked about spirits fiddling with a particular piece of electronic equipment, and quite often the pattern of spontaneous on and off behaviour is confirmed.

Further down the room, Loraine "gets" that someone choked in his own vomit, that a woman's grandmother liked salmon sandwiches and never went out without polishing her shoes, several names of relatives who crossed over, and that someone's mother had ulcerated legs and had finished only half the washing when she died. All of these things are confirmed.

LORNA

Loraine crosses over to an elderly woman in a red coat with snow white hair, and says she has a husband link from the other side. Loraine asks the woman, Lorna, if she wears her husband's watch, and Lorna says that she carries it with her.

Loraine reads that Lorna's husband went very quick, in two days, and tells her that the dream she had of him wasn't a dream. Loraine mentions several names: Harry, Rosemarie, Leonard, Stan, Big Charley, and Little Charley, all people Lorna can place in her past. But when Loraine asks who had the American connection, Lorna doesn't know. She can't think of any of her relatives or close friends who have gone to the U.S.

Loraine re-phrases the question by asking Lorna who might have had a bit of a romance when the American soldiers were in town, and this sweet white-haired lady blushes as red as her coat. With the audience in hysterics, it is the perfect time for an intermission.

During the break the woman seated on my right, Susan, who had a divorce connection that she didn't want to discuss, confides that everything Loraine said to her was true. Her family indeed had a Big Grandad and a Little Grandad, and all the names and medical details Loraine mentioned fit into her family.

Susan tells me that years ago, she lived down the street from Loraine for a while. She said they didn't socialize much, and while Loraine might have seen her children around, she wouldn't have any reason to know about Susan's relatives and events from her past. Susan also confirms the funeral connection and says that so many of her extended family members have passed away lately that she's taken up making funeral wreathes. In her wreaths, she uses nine roses, just as Loraine mentioned.

I ask Susan if she's going to write down questions to put into the hat box, and she says she can't because she needs to be careful. Her daughter is in the audience, on the other side of the room, and there are family issues, particularly about Susan's ex, (her first husband), that she has kept from her daughter. In fact, her daughter knows very little about her biological father, and Susan thinks this is for the best. She didn't realize her daughter would be coming tonight, and frankly, Susan was relieved when her ex didn't come through during her reading.

SALLY

Sally, a woman with sandy grey hair and a flowered zip jumper, stops by to talk to me even though she hasn't received a reading tonight. She explains that she had a private reading a few months ago that made quite an impact.

Before she went to see Loraine, Sally had been to a lot of other mediums, at least sixteen, but none of them had convinced her they were actually in touch with spirits. When she met Loraine, hoping beyond hope to get a message from her departed son, she was doubtful. But when Loraine sat down and started to talk, "Bang! There he was."

Sally tells me that her son's personality came through exactly the same way he had been in life. For the more tangible "proof," Loraine told her his birthday, exactly, and the date of his death, within two days. Then, through Loraine, he thanked Sally for the poem she wrote for his memorial service, which she had done because he had a huge fondness for poetry.

There is very little worse in life than losing a son or daughter, but as Sally explains, that twenty minutes she spent at her private reading with Loraine gave Sally a great release from her grief. Sally is now convinced that death is not the end and feels that Loraine has given her more than she can fully express.

Sally tells me, "All I can say is that I wouldn't be here today if it wasn't for Loraine."

I ask where she would be.

Without hesitation, Sally says, "I would be dead."

I am floored by the frankness and intensity of her response. At the same time, I am a little worried that Sally might be deeply disappointed if her son doesn't come through during the second half of the show.

"Of course I would like him to come through," she tells me. "After all, that's why I've come tonight. But now I know he's all right. If he doesn't come through, it's because he's giving others the chance to come through. That's my boy."

Once again, Sally is a proud mother, and now, not even death can take that from her.

JACK , DELLA, and MANDY

The show resumes and Loraine goes to a row near the middle and says she has someone named Paul on the spirit side. A young man named Jack says it was his mother's cousin. Loraine asks if Paul was in his twenties when he passed and Jack verifies that he was.

Loraine says she also sees Jack's grandfather on the other side and asks if his mother or mother-in-law has come with him tonight.

"Mum-in-law," he says pointing to a woman two seats away.

Loraine switches to the mother-in-law, Mandy, and says she sees a fancy wedding coming up, and it's going to cost a fortune. Loraine asks Mandy if she knows a young man who died in a car accident. Mandy says this happened a long time ago.

Loraine asks Jack and the young woman beside him if they're going to make a baby before or after the wedding. Jack says they'll do it after the wedding. Definitely. He wants a son.

"What's wrong with girls?" asks Loraine. Then she asks if Jack's mother is still alive, and if maybe she's been feeling a little left out of the wedding, and things in general. Jack thinks Loraine might be right about that.

Loraine asks who has the high blood pressure. It is Jack's father, still living. Loraine assures Jack that his father will be fine and will make it to the wedding, even though she senses the wedding won't be this year, but the next.

Della, Jack's fiancé, says the wedding is indeed planned for next year, and that her mother, Mandy, has been helping with the planning. Loraine asks Jack if Mandy is going on the honeymoon as well. Jack says she can come if she wants. Loraine mines this for all it is worth, and the crowd roars.

Then Loraine "sees" decorating going on in Mandy's home, with the whole house torn apart and things everywhere. Mandy admits she has moved everything around to get the house painted, but hasn't managed to get to it done over the past four years.

Loraine asks who is Eileen or Irene, and Mavis. Mandy doesn't know the first name, but Mavis has been gone a while.

"Who lost the cat?" Loraine asks. "And who was married twice? The first one in the family to have a second marriage."

Mandy explains this was her mother.

Loraine says, "She's telling me you need to get the house done before the wedding."

Della and Jack couldn't agree more.

SUSAN'S DAUGHTER, LINDA

On the opposite side of the room towards the back of the hall, Loraine asks if someone knows a Stacy, still on the earth plane. A young woman, Linda, acknowledges that she does. Loraine asks if her friend Stacy recently lost a baby. Linda thinks it is possible, but isn't sure.

Loraine asks Linda if she knows someone named Alan. Linda says it is her mother's brother, still alive.

"Of course he is," Loraine says. "Your grandmother is here and says she doesn't want Alan to join her right away."

Susan, sitting next to me in the front row, whispers to me that Linda is her daughter, and confides that she has decided it would finally be okay if Linda learned a few things about her biological father.

As soon as she says this, on the far side of the room, Loraine asks Linda, "And who is Michael?"

"That was my father's name," Linda tells her.

"Michael says your grandmother didn't come to his funeral, and he says *good,* because at least she's not a fecking hypocrite."

Next to me, Susan rolls her eyes and whispers to me, "That's exactly what he would have said." I can see why Susan divorced him. I have rarely heard such bitter words come from Loraine.

"What an angry man," Loraine says, as much to herself as to the audience. "But Linda, your dad loves you, misses you, and he thinks about you now and then. And with that I'll say God bless."

It seems to me this reading has ended quite abruptly, as soon as the Michael presence showed up. The crowd applauds, but Loraine looks a little shaken. I get the feeling she didn't enjoy linking with Michael's still-angry spirit.

"Sometimes," Loraine explains, "the way they come through gets me in trouble. If they swore in real life, that's how they're likely to come through. If you notice sometimes that my voice changes, it's because I work in trance. I don't have to pause and think a while to get it, it comes to me very fast. If it didn't, my spirit guides would get bored with me."

I doubt that. It's hard to imagine anyone bored with Loraine.

At this point in the show, there is a drawing and a table full of door prizes. Everyone received a numbered ticket stub when they came in, and people win things like chocolates, stuffed animals, or a bottle of wine. It's a cheerful touch and in a three-hour show, it gives Loraine's voice a few moments of rest.

As one woman shows her winning ticket to claim her prize, she gasps.

"This is weird," she says. "I got a sudden chill on my arm and I looked down, and a feather has landed, right on my hand."

"Is it a white feather?" asks Jen, a woman sitting in the second row.

"It is," says the woman as she examines the tiny feather.

Jen smiles. "My auntie told me before she died that if she could, she would try to come through by leaving a white feather."

Later, Jen is still beaming as she tells me that although her other relatives have delivered messages through Loraine before, her auntie Diana was the youngest of her siblings and too shy to speak up in front of a room full of strangers. Jen is thrilled the white feather showed as it did, and sure that it was no coincidence the way it appeared on the woman's hand just as she was claiming her prize. To Jen, even the light-hearted door prize segment of Loraine's show has been infused with meaning.

QUESTIONS - FROM FOOTBALL TO DEATH

Now it is time for Loraine to pick the written questions out of the hat. The first is from Jill, a young woman with dark hair who asks, "Do you approve of Dale?"

Loraine tells Jill that she's got her grandmother here, on her mother's side, who says she likes Dale. She likes him very much. Much better than the last one. Grandma says she's pleased he doesn't snore as much as the last one. But Grandma wants to know what Jill is doing, sleeping with him already.

When the laughter settles down, Loraine tells her that all joking aside, Grandma really likes Dale, and appreciates that Jill was looking at Mum's pictures of her the other day. She asks if Jill showed the pictures to Dale.

Jill nods, looking pleased that Loraine has brought this up.

Loraine picks another question out of the hat. It is from Jack, the young man engaged to Della, and his question asks: "Is he okay? Is that him I feel around me sometimes?"

"Your grandad?" Loraine says. "Of course he's okay, because he came through. He's always around you. In fact, he's one of your spirit guides. Some people have fancy guides, like famous people. As for me, I'm stuck with a dead Egyptian."

When the giggling subsides, Loraine says that along with Ramos, her main spirit guide, tonight she feels a second guide is working with her, although she doesn't know who this one is.

Loraine asks Jack if there is another Jack in the family. He says his other grandfather had the same name.

Loraine asks who the third Jack is, because she sees that there are actually three Jacks in the family.

Jack smiles and admits that there is one more in the family, and it's his dog.

What a family portrait!

Loraine says that his grandfather has met up with his nan, and someone who was married three times. Loraine gives the names Doreen, Peter, Florrie, and Annie, all which make perfect sense to Jack as part of his grandfather's circle of family and friends.

During this break, Jack tells me that he used to be a big sceptic, but after seeing one of Loraine's shows, he's changed his mind. In fact, he has become such a believer that he has come here tonight, despite the fact that he's missing the FA [Football Association] quarter-finals and he's a huge football fan. Apparently, it's a big game between Tottenham and Fulham.

I notice a cell phone not far from Jack's hand, and I ask if he's really missing the scores. Actually, he admits with a sheepish grin, throughout the show he's been sneaking a peek at the score updates.

Loraine takes a few more questions from the hat, and one of the last questions is from Tina, who wants to know, "Will Grandad will be okay?"

Loraine tells Tina that she sees a hospital bed for Grandad, and can tell that he has already had two near death experiences. She feels he's become tired and given up a bit since Christmas.

Tina confirms that Grandad has seemed very down since Christmas. Loraine tells her that Grandad won't go until the cuckoo returns.

Loraine seems confused by her own response. She explains that she doesn't know what it means since she doesn't know that much about birds, and asks the audience when cuckoos return from migration. Someone answers that these birds return in May. Since it is March, that is only two months away. Loraine tells Tina to be happy for every day she has with her grandfather, and she wishes she had something better to tell her.

But the good news, Loraine says, is that death isn't necessarily the end, or something to fear. After all, no one is afraid of being born, and birth is just as traumatic a transition. Perhaps even more so.

I am curious about Loraine's views on death. I see other people leaning forward in their chairs, as well. For someone who "speaks" to people on the other side, this is the first I have heard her talk about the actual experience of being dead.

Loraine relates an experience where she was in such a deep meditative state that she slipped over to the other side. She hadn't meant to, she was just doing a past life regression, hoping that sometime in a past life, she could see if she had been a marvellously flamboyant person. But instead of regressing, she went into the spirit world where they showed her what happens when you die.

As she explains it, she found herself in a sort of waiting room, a place where some spirits are sent back to the earth plane and some go further on. She also was shown a place where people went who had done terrible things in life. It didn't look like the traditional version of Hell. Instead, to Loraine, it looked more like a healing chamber where angry souls could work through their aggressions.

She also saw a separate place where the souls of babies went, and in the distance, she saw her own mother, Maureen. She started to head towards her mother, but her spirit guide, Ramos, who she could finally see clearly, told her not to go. Loraine says she argued with Ramos but he told her that if she went that far, she wouldn't be able to go back. Loraine found it so peaceful that she wanted to stay. She wanted so much to talk to her mother, but the next moment she found herself pushed back, and waking up in her body.

She recalls feeling angry at the time because it was so peaceful that she didn't want to be sent back to the physical world.

Her experience sounds similar to something my father told me when he was hospitalized with stomach cancer. At one point his heart stopped, and there were a number of tense minutes before they got it going again. Later, when he revived, he told me he had found himself in a place that was so wonderful and peaceful, that if there had been a switch on the wall to allow him to stay, he would have pushed it. Instead, he returned to the world of the living for another week before his heart gave out the second and final time. But during that week, he had no fear of dying.

My father had always had a life-long fear of death, but after that near-death experience, in his final week, facing a serious operation which should have been the scariest time of all, he was not afraid. It would be hard to imagine a bigger transformation, and it was a huge blessing to see him at peace, ready to embrace whatever happened.

Chapter 9

BRENTWOOD
March 2010

On a crisp day at the end of March, I drive north-east of London, and find myself in the packed aisles of the Mind Body Soul Exhibition at Brentwood. At noon, I head upstairs to the workshop room to get a good seat for Loraine's 12:30 p.m. show. With my notepad and tape recorder ready, I stake out a spot on the far right seat in the front row. For this show, I have also borrowed a video camera. My friend Sue B. has come with me today to help out. She sets up the video camera near the back to film the whole room. I will use the video later (see Appendix II) to compare against my notes and tape recording, a triple check to ensure my account is accurate.

Soon, there is a good crowd of people, all wondering what's going to happen.

Loraine arrives, a big smile on her face, and notices a boy, about seven years old, in the second row.

"Hello, luv, what's your name?"

"Jimmy."

"Well, Jimmy, you may have to hold your ears from time to time, because if the spirits swore while they were alive, that's how they'll come through today."

Jimmy nods, pleased to be noticed.

Loraine asks, "Does your mum swear?"

Jimmy giggles and nods.

Loraine smiles. "Then we'll be all right. Hello, everyone! The way it works is that the spirits come through my main guide, Ramos. Hopefully he'll be here, but I'm not worried. He's been around all day. He loves us Essex girls. In fact, he loves all girls, actually. He was a big tall Egyptian, and sometimes you'll see me touch my ear. That's him, giving me kisses in my ear. Can you all uncross your legs and close your eyes a moment, and I'll put lots of light around you for good energy. Now, when I come to you, I don't want any clues, but do speak up and give me your name. Because we're all bloody nosey, aren't we? And we like to know other people's gossip. But if you've got a secret you don't want out, give me a signal to *cut*. But chances are I've already said it anyway. We're all here to have a good laugh, although talking to spirits can be a little sad. Anyway, when I come to you, speak up and give us your name."

After reading a woman named Nicky, Loraine walks down the middle aisle and stops by a couple sitting together.

CHRIS AND PAULA

The man identifies himself as Chris. Loraine says she feels he is good at analysing things, and that he has lost his dad. Chris says no.

"Then I've got your grandad here. He's showing me a hospital bed. He went very fast at the end."

Chris agrees that this is what happened. Loraine turns to the woman beside him, who identifies herself as Paula.

"Did you lose your mum?" Loraine asks.

Paula seems confused, then answers, "It was a long time ago."

"Well, she's still bloody dead."

Everyone laughs, including Paula.

Loraine adds, "I will say that your mum had a very sad life. I do feel that you had a 'mum' that brought you up, and a mum that birthed you. And the mum that birthed you had a tragic end. I see her all around you. And she tells me that she likes Chris. If she was still alive, she's telling me she'd ask if there was another of him. But now, I'm seeing your nan around you. And she knew a whole lot more about you than your mum ever did."

"Yes," Paula says.

"And your grandad as well," Loraine continues. "Because I do feel that your grandparents played a very important role in your life and bringing you up."

"Yes, they did."

"They're telling me they loved you very much. Now, I'm seeing a change in jobs for you. Do you work with very important people?"

"I have done."

"I see you working with important people. Actually, I'm not sure if they're really important, or if they just think they are. You get what I mean?"

Paula does.

"I'm seeing Big Ben," Loraine says. "Did you work near Big Ben?"

Again, confirmation.

Loraine continues. "These important people who worked near Big Ben, I feel they'll be in contact with you to work with them again. And it was bloody good money, wasn't it?"

"It was indeed."

"Your grandad liked you working there," says Loraine. "I'm not sure why... Were they politicians that you worked with?"

Paula looks uncomfortable. "Close."

"What do you mean, close?"

"Government workers," Paula explains.

"Same thing. They do feel up their own... that they're important."

Everyone laughs.

Loraine concludes the reading by saying, "They tell me that you're wonderful, and I will leave you with their love and say God Bless."

The room applauds.

MARGARET AND JANE

Loraine asks the audience if anyone is bored.

The audience roars, "No!"

"Good," Loraine says. "I'm glad my guide is doing his job today. Now, I want to come here." Loraine stops before two women. They identify themselves as Margaret and her sister-in-law Jane.

"Hello, girls. I see a man standing between you. Who's lost their father?"

It is Margaret.

"And who played the guitar?"

Margaret, again.

Loraine puts her hands on her hips. "Then, can you learn to do it properly? They're telling me that all you ever did was strum away. And who is David?"

Margaret explains that David is her brother.

"Your father wants to validate David. And also something to do with the circus. Clowns."

"My father was something of an entertainer."

"He tells me he went quite quickly."

"Yes."

"And who had the cancer?"

"My mum."

"And she's passed?"

"No."

"Then this isn't her. Who else had cancer?"

"Her mum."

"As she comes in, she's really crying. Because she really loved life. She's giving me a cup of tea and a cake. She did like to feed people, didn't she?"

"She did."

"I'm seeing a very nice Sunday roast. Now, who is Eena?"

Margaret doesn't know. Loraine isn't ready to give it up.

"Eena? Leena? Enna?" she asks. "It's a really weird name."

Margaret looks confused.

"Then hold on to that name," Loraine says, "and have a think about it."

"My father had thirteen siblings," Margaret explains, "and I didn't know them all."

"Someone was a sailor," Loraine says. "He went off to sea."

Margaret shrugs. "Could be one of my nan's brothers."

"She's telling me there were five that went off to war, and only three that returned. They could have been cousins, but they were all part of the family."

Margaret doesn't know.

"Your best link is your dad," Loraine says, "and he's telling me about teeth. Who needs to see their dentist?"

"Me," says Margaret.

"And who has a bad back? You or someone else."

"My mum."

"Thank you, because your father's rubbing down my back. And I thought he was just being friendly."

Margaret enjoys the joke. Loraine continues. "He says he loves you and misses you. And also he says you are thinking of a holiday, and you're thinking of two places. He wants me to tell you to go to the furthest afield place. Because he wants to go there with you. And he says it won't cost you a penny, because now that he's in the spirit world, he can go with you for nothing. Now who had all the bloody shoes? A wardrobe full of shoes."

"That would be Mum."

"Everything's all in the wardrobe. You wanted to take it all to Oxfam, but she won't part with anything."

"No, she won't," says Margaret.

Loraine continues. "I do feel there's a lot of 'old toot.' Now there's a funny word, isn't it? Old toot."

Margaret explains. "That was one of my dad's sayings. He was always complaining about too much 'old toot'."

Loraine gives the name Bill and Mary. She asks if Mary was her father's aunt, the one that read the tea leaves.

Margaret admits that's all true.

"And tell Mum your dad's been playing with the TV. Has the TV been acting up?" Loraine asks.

"Yes, she can't get her digital to work."

"It's your father," Loraine says. "He doesn't want her to watch it. He says he's been playing tricks on her."

Everyone laughs, although I know that Loraine is actually being serious here.

"But he's getting a bit solemn now," Loraine continues. "He's talking about your brother, your brother is still alive?"

Margaret nods.

"He doesn't really give your mum that much time," Loraine says. "He won't do anything with her. But your dad tells me she's done nothing wrong. And it's almost like your brother can't bear to go in that house any more. It's like his head is in the sand."

Margaret nods vigorously.

"I also feel like your brother's a little bit depressed," Loraine tells her. "And Dad says you need to go around to his house and box his ears."

Margaret shakes her head. "He's a big boy to do that."

"Then get your friend to do it!"

Jane laughs along with everyone else, and Loraine wraps up the reading and moves further down the room.

WENDY

Loraine approaches a woman further down the aisle. "And my next victim is...?"

"Wendy."

"Hello, Wendy. Do they call you Bendy Wendy?"

"No," Wendy answers.

"Are you sure?" Loraine turns to Wendy's friends sitting next to her. "Well? Do you?"

"No," they insist.

"All right," Loraine continues. "Wendy, I do see quite a few lights around you. Your family is not as loud as most of the people who have come through today, do you understand? I've got your nan here. She comes through as sheepish, but she wants you to know that she's often around you. Now who's having trouble with their feet?"

It is Wendy.

"Your nan wants to validate that she had trouble with her feet as well. She's also giving me a connection with a black dog. Who lost the black dog?"

"My brother."

"Your nan wants to say she's got the smelly mutt with her. And it's got bad wind."

Wendy laughs.

"Your nan was lovely," Loraine says. "Did you lose your dad? Because I've got Dad here, and he was scared to come through, but here he is. Your dad tells me you panic about everybody. Your dad says you've got to stop panicking about everything, especially at Christmas. Do you understand?"

Wendy nods.

"And something to do with Christmas presents that you never give people. Do you understand?"

Wendy agrees that she has forgotten to give gifts she has wrapped for people.

Loraine gives her the names Albert, Frank, and James. Wendy can't validate them but she says her father had a big family and she didn't know them all.

Loraine says, "Your dad wants to validate that he was around the house the other day. And somebody needs to change the light bulb upstairs. It's been like that for ages."

Wendy nods in agreement.

"He says how can you have a wee in the dark? You're asking for a bloody accident."

Wendy laughs.

"And he's talking about the loo brush with a duck in it."

"Oh, yes. I had one like that."

"And with that silly thing standing in it, somebody broke it. But your dad is a lovely guy. Can you take the name of George? And Edie?"

Wendy can. Loraine also mentions Joyce, Jean or Joan, and Elizabeth, maybe known as Betsy. And a John. Wendy confirms each one of these names.

"There ARE a lot of them over there," Loraine says as she wraps up the reading.

As Loraine moves away to read someone else, she stops mid-stride.

"I'm getting the name Paul," she says. "He was a young man who hung himself. I hate to work this way, to get a connection without knowing who I am connecting to. Can anyone take a Paul who killed himself?"

No one moves.

"He's very upset that no one remembers him," says Loraine. "He's trying very hard to come through. Does anyone know a Paul like this?"

Again, no one responds.

"Then I'll have to let him go," says Loraine as she walks towards the front of the room.

PAULINE AND SUE

"Next?" she says, and stops beside two women. "Who's lost their dad?"

"I have," says the one on the right, who identifies herself as Sue.

"Your dad tells me that you're very spiritual," Loraine tells her. "A psychic yourself."

"So I've been told," Sue answers.

"He's showing me tarot cards. Have you got tarot cards?" Sue says that she does.

"I can tell that you have a psychic talent, and when I do my talent circles, I would like you to come to develop your talent. Most people pay for this training, but I won't charge you. You've got that much potential."

"Thank you," says Sue.

"Your father is giving you a big hug. Your dad's mum was nice, and your mother's mum was even nicer."

"True."

"Your dad went on a train trip. The Orient Express. Do you understand?"

Sue nods.

"I'm also picking up a connection with the month of June. Do you have a connection with June?"

"My birthday."

"And I'm also seeing the ninth of November?" Loraine says.

"The day before, my grandmother was born."

Loraine smiles. "She says your father was born with lovely lungs, and big feet. Bloody big feet. Size eleven?"

"Might have been," Sue tells her.

"Your father sends his love, and your grandad, too. Who has the lower back pain?"

"Me," says Sue.

"Your dad says 'when are you going to get your life sorted out?' He says he's doesn't mean it, he's just repeating what Mom always says to you to wind you up."

Next to Sue is her mother, Pauline, who answers, "I do say that."

Loraine turns back to Sue. "Your dad says you worry about losing your mum, but you don't have to. She'll be here another twenty years, at least." Then Loraine turns to Pauline. "He's also telling me that the little robin you saw was him. Do you understand?"

Pauline nods.

"He says you're thinking of getting a new car. A sports car?"

Pauline admits that she is.

"He says don't get a red one."

Pauline frowns. "But I was thinking of red."

"He says don't get a red one, get yourself a nice silver or blue. Maybe a Fiesta. Or a little KA car."

Pauline doesn't look impressed.

"Whatever you get," Loraine concludes, "be happy, and safe and with that I'll say God bless. Thank you everyone for coming to my show. Can you all close your eyes a moment, as I don't want to send you out with your energy open."

Some people look confused, and Loraine explains. "One time at a show at Kempton Park, a mother came through who was really angry, and she made the windows rattle, and the energy in the room was really cracking. I wouldn't want to mess about with her. Anyway, the next time the woman was in the audience, the mother came through again. I kept thinking I am not going to talk to this mother, but the spirit kept pinching me, all up and down my back. Later, at a reading, the mother came through again but this time, she was calmer. So the spirits do change, and calm down a little bit if we're lucky. But you do meet some funny people, and spirits are just people who have crossed over, so today I want to close you out safely. I will leave you all by thanking the spirits who have made contact with us, with love and light. And I wish everyone the best in their lives."

This is the first time I have seen Loraine close a show with such a precaution. I am wondering if Loraine felt an energy presence with unfinished business. The audience doesn't seem to notice as the people applaud and the session ends. Although Loraine has been talking about the greatest sorrows in life, about death and those we grieve for, the mood is light and joyful as everyone gets up to leave. Outside in the hallway, I talk to as many people who got readings as I can.

The first people I talk to after the show are Chris and Paula. Paula confirms that her birth mother did meet a tragic end, and that she was raised by her grandparents. She tells me that she used to work near Big Ben, and she pulls out her i-phone and shows me a picture of Big Ben that she took outside her work place. She explains that her job there involved both politicians and government officials.

Chris explains that he is indeed analytical, as Loraine suggested, and that what she said about his grandfather was true. They come to see Loraine's shows whenever they can, and tell me they always leave with a smile.

I notice there is more than a smile on their faces. They are shining with an inner glow. I look around and see that most people coming out of the room look the same way. No one seems complacent, no one looks bored. The people are leaving the session with their spirits lifted higher than when they went in.

For the believers, there is a flutter of joy. For the unsure, they leave with hope. For the still-sceptical, they leave with food for thought.

But no one leaves empty. This is Loraine's gift.

After talking with Chris and Pauline, a woman named Carol introduces herself and says, "I did know a Paul who hung himself." She explains that she was too uncomfortable to talk about the details of his death in front of a whole room of people. She hopes Paul will understand. While she felt unsure about discussing his death in a public venue, she wants me to know she has not forgotten him.

Then I catch up with Margaret who says that all the names that Loraine mentioned were indeed relatives. She didn't understand the name Eena at first, but now she recalls her father talking about his aunt Eena.

Margaret knows that several great-uncles went off to war, but she can't validate the exact number, or the number who returned.

She also relates that her father often complained about her mother's "old toot." It was one of his favourite expressions. She explains that Loraine not only got his phrasing right, but also the exact essence of his personality. She is not surprised to hear that the reason her mother can't get her new digital TV to work may have something to do with her impish father. He was a practical joker in life, and since his death, there have been several mysterious incidents, including a ringing telephone that can't be found, that have made her feel he may not be too far away.

Then Margaret validates that she has indeed been debating between two different places for her next holiday. I ask if the reading helped her make up her mind. She says that is has, because now she's decided to go to both.

Unfortunately, the reference to Margaret's brother is not so light-hearted. She explains that ever since her father died five years ago, her brother David has been paralysed with denial and sorrow, and has been unable to face his mother in all that time. It is a source of great sadness and regret that he can not be strong enough to support his mother in her time of need.

Next I talk to Wendy, who confirms the information about her brother's smelly black dog. Wendy tells me that that the names Loraine gave her were spot on, as she had an Uncle Albert, an Uncle Jim, an Aunt Edith, and currently has a broken bulb in the upstairs bathroom. She quite enjoyed hearing that her father knew about the broken light bulb in the bathroom, and the comical loo brush that had stood in its china cradle until the handle broke.

Wendy says she has had readings with other mediums before, but none of them gave such specifics as Loraine.

As I take a photo of Wendy with Margaret and Jane, all three beaming with satisfaction, I realize that Jane didn't actually get a reading.

"I'm not disappointed," Jane says. "It is enough to see so much confirmed for Margaret. And if nothing else, I've been well-entertained."

Finally, I catch up with Sue and her mother, Pauline. It was Pauline's husband and Sue's father who came through very strongly, and they felt honoured and touched that he had. Pauline explains that she really does wind Sue up by asking when she's going to get her life sorted out, and was delighted to hear Loraine using the same exact words. It is a comfort to hear that her husband is still a part of the family banter.

Pauline also explains that her husband had a real fondness for robins, and when Loraine mentioned the robin, she knew exactly what it meant. A few days before, Pauline had seen a robin land on the exact spot where her husband's ashes were buried. At the time, she knew it was a message from him and it gave her a sense of peace. Loraine's acknowledgement of the robin was an affirmation of what she already knew in her heart.

As for the new car in her future, Pauline has now decided that instead of going for the red colour she originally wanted, or the blue that Loraine said her husband preferred, Pauline has decided to keep everyone happy and compromise right down the middle, and get herself a nice sporty purple.

Pauline also shares that she has recently had a private reading with Loraine, and tells me she received two memorable messages from her husband at that reading. The first message that came through was that yes, there is indeed a God. No specifics, just that God exists. The second message was that Pauline should really learn how to cook.

"Cook?" I ask. "What kind of cook are you?"

Her face blushes peach pink. "Terrible."

NICOLE

A few days after the Brentwood show, I was contacted by Nicole, a young woman who had a private reading with Loraine that day, and it changed her life.

Nicole's mother died when she was just sixteen, leaving Nicole and her younger sister feeling lost and alone in the world. For ten years, Nicole has been searching for answers, for something that would tell her one way or another if her mother was still with her.

As Nicole approached twenty-six, she had just faced another milestone -- her wedding, and now that she was beginning her own family, it was even more important to know if her mother's presence was near.

Although Nicole had been to numerous mediums and psychics, she always went away feeling incomplete, as if something were missing. When her new mother-in-law told her that she really should book a reading with Loraine, Nicole was sceptical, but she went, just in case.

As the reading progressed, Nicole was very careful not to say too much, just a simple "yes" or "no," to make sure she didn't give away any specifics about herself.

But after that twenty-minute reading with Loraine, Nicole came out of that session a changed woman. For the first time in ten years, she felt satisfied. That burning hunger, that terrible empty pain of not knowing, was gone.

Loraine explained that the white feathers that floated around Nicole, sometimes hovering stationary above her, were gifts from her mother. Loraine described sixteen names, very specific names, all from Nicole's or her mother's past. These were names that only she and her sister could have possibly known.

Loraine knew that Nicole's grandmother had died four days before Nicole's wedding, and deeply regretted not being there in person.

Loraine also knew that the family had grieved so much that they cut off all contact with Nicole and her younger sister, casting them even further adrift in a sea of loneliness as they struggled to grow and mature, motherless, and try to come to terms with their place in the world.

And when Loraine said, "Tell Maisy Moo that I love her," Nicole knew that there was only one person who used that term of endearment. It wasn't officially her name. It wasn't anything like her name. Only one other person had ever used it, and hearing it so long after her mother's death lighted a bonfire in Nicole's heart.

As Nicole says, if you have lost someone that important, you cling to everything. You paint every little scrap of memory with so much feeling, and squeeze it so tight that it no longer becomes a memory but a hope of what a memory could be. But when those treasured fragments of memories fade, or become so distorted you can't even recall what is real and what is the dream, you can lose your faith, and become an unbeliever.

That twenty minutes with Loraine had given Nicole the validation she had sought for so long, that her mother's presence was still with her, and that her love was so strong that even death could not stop it.

For Nicole to finally have that comfort, that overpowering sense of peace at last, was an experience beyond words.

Not everyone has such a powerful reading. Not everyone has such a need for resolution, or a desire to even consider exploring a connection on the other side. But as Nicole says, it is easy to disbelieve something you have not experienced.

Fortunately for Nicole, she had enough faith to continue to hope that she might someday find that genuine sense of connection. And lucky for her that Loraine has not shied away from her gift, but has used it generously. As Loraine herself says, she may not be the world's best clairvoyant, because at the end of the day, there will always be someone out there who is better, whoever you are or whatever you do.

But Loraine knows that she can hold her head high. She does what she does to the best of her abilities, and for all the right reasons. She knows her efforts are well spent if she can help give people the courage and confidence to go on, and reconnect them with family and dear friends through the unbreakable bonds of love. After all, as John (on pp. 37) from the West Sussex Show said, that's what it's all about.

Chapter 10

THE LINTON SHOW
September 2010

I didn't see Loraine again for five months, and in that time, a lot of things happened in her life. For one thing, Loraine's house burned down. No one was in it at the time -- a miracle -- so no one was lost.

It was a sheer accident that everyone was out when the fire struck. Loraine was at the hospital with her sons Danny and Billy because Billy had sprained his ankle. Emmaleigh was out shopping with a cousin, Amelia was at school, and Kayleigh was at a theatre class. Loraine had no idea the house was at risk, and no sense of pending fire danger. However, her daughter Kayleigh, who has displayed the most psychic talent of Loraine's children so far, had been sensing smoke and fumes in the house for a few months before the fire occurred.

As Loraine explains, while she can read messages for others, her own life is mostly a surprise. This is why, she says, she's been married three times. She is free to make her own mistakes, as many as she wants, and as she attests, it is a freedom she liberally applies.

The fire wasn't the only setback because around that time, the marriage to Mark started to show signs of strain.

And if all this wasn't enough to juggle, Loraine had an operation scheduled that year that required a seven hour procedure. This was not an easy thing to face given that Loraine had previously proven to be susceptible to excessive bleeding.

Before the operation, Loraine met a doctor, the neurosurgeon Hisham Daghenstani, who helped her build up her strength for the surgery. The operation was lengthy but when it was over and Loraine finally woke up from the anaesthesia, still groggy, she called Hisham. As they spoke on the telephone, she told Hisham that his father had just visited her and given her a drink made of condensed grape juice to help her heal. For about an hour, she described his father's vineyard in Damascus in clear detail, and told Hisham how his mother had wrapped a shawl around her shoulders to keep her warm.

The next day, when Hisham arrived at the Hospital to check up on Loraine, she didn't recall anything about the conversation. She couldn't even remember that she had called him at all.

But Hisham remembered. His father, who had risked his life saving freedom fighters during the French Vichy Regime's occupancy of Syria, had been very proud of the thick grape drink he used to make from his vineyard in Damascus. But he hadn't made this drink in a very long time because Hisham's father had died in 1969. And when Hisham's mother went blind several years after that, the last thing she did was to knit Hisham a shawl, exactly like the one Loraine described.

In all the years that his father has been gone, Hisham has never had any indication or feeling that his father's spirit was present. He has not even had any memorable dreams of him. But from the details that Loraine told him when she was still semi-delirious from the surgery, Hisham is now convinced that both his parents are still with him, since they had come to comfort his friend in a crucial time, during her lengthy surgery.

By September of 2010, Loraine was fully recovered and putting on shows again with her usual vigour. On a brisk Autumn day, I drove up the M11 to catch her show in Linton, not far from Cambridge. Here's what happened that day.

AMY AND DON

I arrive in time for the start of Loraine's one hour demonstration show. The first person Loraine comes to is a woman called Amy, who is sitting next to a man named Don. Loraine explains that Amy's grandmother is here, and she really approves of Don. Loraine sees a little boy with blue eyes who died very young and asks Amy if she lost an infant or had a late miscarriage. Amy confirms it was a miscarriage. Loraine says the little boy wants her to know his eyes were very blue.

Loraine then asks Don if he just left five years of a

disastrous relationship with another woman. He acknowledges that this is true. Loraine says she has Don's father here, who never bothered to be a good dad, and his grandfather who was in the army and worked as a mechanic alongside his friend Roger the Fish. Don knows his grandfather was in the army but doesn't know what he did or who his friends were.

Loraine gives the names Paula and David, and Amy verifies them as members of her family who have passed on. Then Loraine says Amy's grandmother wants to know when Amy will marry Don. Grandmother says to stop putting up barriers because the perfect man is not out there, except for Don. Then, according to Loraine, Amy's grandfather also chimes in from the other side to support a wedding, and says Amy and Don would be married already if Don wasn't getting what he wanted. Grandfather "says" that in his day, it was a closed shop and you had to get married to get what you wanted from a relationship.

Afterwards, Amy tells me that she felt uncomfortable with the reading because it made her feel like a tart. Since she isn't married to Don, she really didn't need everyone in that room to know how far her relationship with Don had progressed.

Don stands up for his woman's honour and vigorously agrees. He says Loraine would be better suited for a blue comedy routine instead of a medium show. This is the first time a couple has complained to me about their readings. However, neither one denies anything Loraine said, and seem to be annoyed because it was *too* true. Loraine does issue a "health warning" that her shows are for people over eighteen. I would also advise caution to people who have secrets they don't want revealed. If that's the case, a private reading might be more suitable. Once Loraine gets started, you just don't know what might come out, and neither does she.

JOAN AND JANICE

Next, Loraine comes to a woman named Joan. Loraine asks who was lost at sea. Joan doesn't know who that could be. Loraine then asks who died from cancer and Joan says it was her husband. Loraine tells Joan that her husband is with the little lad. Then Loraine asks who rubbed his hand after he died and kissed him on the nose. Joan verifies that she did this. Loraine says they almost forgot to put socks on him at his funeral, and they only got them on him at the last minute. Joan is visibly stunned to hear this and explains that she was the only one who knew about that.

Loraine relates that she feels Joan is still angry about her husband's death. Joan is shaken to hear this spoken out loud and her emotions become quite apparent. Loraine explains that her husband didn't want to go and leave her, that she was the love of his life and he was always faithful to her, but he always knew in his heart that he would go first. By now, Loraine and Joan are both crying, and many of the audience members are close to tears as well.

Loraine gives Joan a string of names, about seven, and Joan says they are all close relatives.

Loraine then turns to Janice, sitting beside Joan, and says she sees a special relationship with butterflies.

Loraine asks who went yellow with cancer, but Janice doesn't know who that could be.

Then Loraine asks about Elsie, and Janice explains that Else was her aunt who died during the war.

After the session is over, Joan and Janice track down Loraine at her booth to thank her for the reading. It is at least half an hour since the reading but Joan is still stunned. As she relates, that very morning, she had hoped beyond hope that her husband would come through and confirm it was really him by telling her that he had the boy with him. Those are the words she needed to hear to believe it was really him and not some trick. And indeed, that is what Loraine said.

Joan tells me that everything Loraine related, except for the person lost at sea, were things she had been "asking" her husband about. Joan explains that hearing her questions answered, by a complete stranger who shouldn't know anything about her, has overwhelmed her in the best possible way. She feels amazed and privileged that Loraine has shared her gift and given her such a powerful validation of her husband's continued presence in her life.

Janice is delighted for her friend. Her own message, concerning the butterfly connection, also touched a very special chord in her life. As Janice explains, butterflies follow her around, and often alight on the clothes of a very dear loved one she has lost. Loraine's mention of butterflies was probably the most meaningful thing she could have said to Janice, and despite the brevity of the message, it couldn't have been more potent.

As Joan and Janice thank Loraine for the messages they received, they are nearly in tears all over again as they struggle to express the depth of their gratitude.

BEVERLY

After Loraine has finished reading Joan and Janice, she walks through the audience to see who she will be drawn to next. As she comes down the aisle between the rows of chairs, a woman in the second row, Beverly, gasps in surprise.

"Did you see it?" Loraine asks.

"Yes," says Beverly. "It went right past your head."

Loraine points just above her left shoulder. "Right here, was it?"

Beverly nods. "That's exactly where it was. And then it went past you. Behind you."

Loraine explains to the crowd. "That was my spirit guide. He says he likes you because you saw him. Not everyone can."

She's right about that. No one else in the room saw it.

After the session, I catch up with Beverly to ask her about her experience.

"It was a grey-white mist," she explains, "and it shot by the left side of Loraine's head."

I ask Beverly if she is a medium herself, or if there is some reason she might have been able to see what she did. She explains that she is in training, and has seen things like this before, usually large grey orbs but sometimes in different colours. From its height, she says Loraine's spirit guide seemed to be very tall. Then she adds, "I don't really know if her spirit guide is a man or woman, but I got the sense of a very big man."

This coincides with Loraine's description of Ramos, her main spirit guide, as a very tall man.

QUESTIONS

Towards the end of the hour, an audience member asks Loraine if she hears from animal spirits. Loraine explains that sometimes a spirit on the other side might tell her they've got the dog or some other animal with them, but she herself doesn't pick up on animal energies. There are clairvoyants that can do that, but Loraine explains that she is not one of them.

Regarding animal spirits, Loraine feels that when a dog dies, if it returns for another life, that it will come back again as a dog, and not as another animal or a human. As far as she can tell, animals don't "upgrade" to something else. If they return, she thinks they return as the same type of creature.

Someone asks if Loraine hears messages all the time, and if it interferes with her daily life. She says that she usually doesn't, and that most of the time, her life is just as normal as it is for anyone else. But sometimes she gets a message when she isn't expecting it. She explains that a few days ago, she was in a shop looking at shoes. There was a woman nearby, about twenty-five, and suddenly Loraine "saw" a baby and received a message to tell the woman that her baby daughter was happy in the spirit world.

Loraine felt uncomfortable about walking up to this woman, a perfect stranger, and telling her that she had a message from her baby daughter, but the message was so strong that she had to comply.

The woman was surprised, and told Loraine that she felt responsible for her baby's death, since the baby had a medical condition and only lived nine hours. The woman was utterly shocked to get a message from her baby girl. It was the exact thing she needed to her to let go of the burden of guilt for not giving her daughter a healthier body.

Loraine explains that when she's not working, she trusts her spirit guides not to bombard her with messages unless it's particularly important. She thinks of herself as a lazy clairvoyant because as she puts it, she often doesn't bother to shut down her chakras [centres of life energy] after readings. Instead, she leaves that to her spirit guides to handle. With six children, she doesn't have time to invest in lengthy rituals to become receptive to messages, or to turn them off. The way she sees it, that is the spirit guide's job to make the connection. They come down to the earth plane to meet her energy; she doesn't go to them. All she does is remain open to the process, and her spirit guides do the rest. For her, this is the way it works.

PAULINE AND SUE, AGAIN

The last people Loraine reads are two women I recognize from a previous show, Pauline and Sue. They wave hello to me, delighted that Loraine has stopped in front of them once again.

"Are you together?" Loraine asks. "Is this your mum?"

They nod.

"I have your father and husband here."

Their heads bob in unison.

"Do you remember your pet rabbit?" Loraine asks Pauline. "The one that died? Well, your father confesses. You ate it."

Pauline was not expecting that.

Loraine continues. "Do you have your husband's picture in a lover frame?"

Pauline explains that the frame that displays her husband's picture is shaped like a heart.

"Was his name Syd?"

Pauline says that it was.

"Who is Flo, or Florrie? The one who read the tea leaves?"

Pauline says it was her aunt, Flo.

"She has a confession as well. She says when she was reading the tea leaves, she made it all up. But the funny thing is, she was always right! So that's still a form of psychic abilities."

Loraine says that the strange banging noises that come out of the TV are not mechanical problems, it is from Syd. This is something Loraine also said at the previous show. Then she gives a string of names: Penny, Vi, Fred, George, Irene, Charlie, and all are verified.

Loraine says that Syd often sits with Pauline when it's nice and quiet, and with that he sends his love.

After the reading, I ask Pauline and Sue how they felt about being read again. Pauline explains they had just come to enjoy the show and were not expecting her husband to come through again. After her first reading with Loraine, she no longer needs any more proof that he is around her. But of course it is nice when he drops in.

Pauline says that this time, her husband repeated some of the same things he "said" the last time, but he added a few more details and little touches.

I remembered what Pauline told me before, that he had left her with two particular messages, about the existence of God and her cooking, and I ask how the cooking is coming along.

"Well," Pauline says, "the good news is that I've gone out and got myself a brand new kitchen. But I'm still a terrible cook."

Chapter 11

QUESTIONS AND ANSWERS

I've been collecting questions to ask Loraine and have compiled a list. I finally get the chance to run them by her. Here are those questions along with her responses.

QUESTION: Does being a medium create any special problems in your life?

LORAINE: I was born with my gift and have always had it. I really can't imagine what it would be like without it. For me, it's not a problem at all. I don't usually get messages when I'm out and about, shopping or driving or buying groceries or getting on with my daily activities. In other words, it doesn't normally interfere with my life.

QUESTION: Do you ever receive messages in different languages?

LORAINE: Spirits use a universal language. There is only one language "up there" in the spirit world, so there is no language barrier. I only speak English, but I can get messages from a friend or relative who has passed over that might have spoken a different language during their life. Sometimes, a word or phrase comes through in their language, especially if it is something that has significance to the person who is being read, something specific they can recognize and need to hear in order to verify the message.

QUESTION: How do you deal with people who are sceptical about life after death?

LORAINE: The funny thing is that sometimes the biggest sceptics can become the biggest believers. One time a woman came to a reading, insisting that she didn't believe any of it. Within ten minutes, she was sobbing her eyes out, so happy to be reconnected with her loved ones who had crossed.

But there are people who come to my shows or get a reading that still don't believe. If they don't believe, or really don't want to, it's not my job to convince them. There's no point in that. I feel it's my job to deliver the messages I am given. What the person does with a message is up to them. I do feel that there are some people who don't want to learn. Maybe it just isn't their path to learn at this time, or be open to the process. We each have our own path to walk, and all paths are different.

QUESTION: Do you get messages about danger?

LORAINE: Sometimes I do. There was one woman I had read a few times who was pregnant with twins. One day when her pregnancy was well-advanced, as I was driving, I got a sudden urge to call her and tell her to go to the hospital right away. She was confused as everything in her pregnancy was going just fine. I encouraged her to go check it out just the same. She went for a scan and they found out that there was something wrong with the flow of blood in her babies. The hospital did an emergency c-section and performed a blood transfusion on both babies. After the transfusion, the babies were fine. The hospital told her that if they hadn't gotten them out when they did, and transfused them with new blood, within a few minutes both babies would have died.

But I don't always get messages like that, not even for myself. Last year, my house burned down and I didn't get any warning at all. Fortunately, we were away and no one was hurt.

QUESTION: Can you control what sort of messages you receive?

LORAINE: I can ask specific questions that a person has, but the answers come from my spirit guides. Ramos is always there but sometimes others join him. When that happens, my accuracy usually goes up and things come to me even faster. But I have no control over what they tell me. I can only trust that what they say is what the person needs to hear at that moment.

Someone asked me once why the spirits don't they tell us how to cure cancer, or end world hunger. But spirits don't become saints or geniuses just because they've crossed over. Your aunt Shirley is still going to be your aunt Shirley even after she's crossed over. If she was a baker in this life, she's not going to instantly become a brain surgeon on the other side.

QUESTION: Do souls reconnect on the other side?

LORAINE: Just as they do on Earth, souls belong to families, or soul clusters. Have you ever met someone you felt comfortable with right away? You might have encountered their soul before and been friends in a previous life. On the same token, there are people you instantly dislike. It could be that this person did something bad to you in a different life. Souls travel in clusters, and tend to come back together if they choose. Your mother in this life might have been your son or your brother in an earlier life. Gender and age don't matter. What is important is the bond of love.

But you don't have to remain together. In the spirit world, your soul is free to join with other souls outside of your earthly family line, if you choose. This is why the marriage vows say "until death do us part." We are under no obligation to remain with a spouse after death if we would rather move on. Just as we are free to choose our friends and associates in this world, we are free to choose who to be with in the next.

QUESTION: Can spirits affect objects or people in the physical world?

LORAINE: Spirits are a form of energy, and energy can affect things on the earth plane. I have seen spirits affect electrical circuits. They can make small appliances such as lights, TVs, or radios go off and on. I have even seen electric appliances turn on, all by themselves, that weren't even plugged in.

I have also seen windows rattle and shake when a particularly angry spirit was present. Fortunately, that doesn't happen very often, and the spirits are not allowed to cause harm to us here in the physical world. I have asked Ramos about this several times, and he says it is simply not permitted for spirits to cause harm to us in the physical world.

QUESTION: Is psychic ability always transmitted through the women of a family?

LORAINE: In my family, it was always the women who were known for having "the gift." But men can have it, as well. My two sons Billy and Danny have psychic ability, but they haven't chosen to develop it. At least, not yet.

QUESTION: When you do readings, you barely look at the clock. But you always finish on time. How do you stay on schedule?

LORAINE: "They" tell me when it's time to wind up a reading or a show. By myself, I am not so organized and on-time in my daily life.

QUESTION: Have you ever been wrong on a prediction?

LORAINE: I don't know, really. I do think that the timing might not be right. I might say something will happen but it might not happen for years. Time isn't the same in the spirit world as it is here. Up there, they can go backwards and forwards in time. It's no problem to them.

And there are certain things a person might be guided to do, but we have free will, so an individual might choose not to act on it. For example, a person might be guided to go work in a medical clinic in Africa. This might be their pathway to do that, but they could decide not to go. In that case, they wouldn't be fulfilling their destiny. Nothing says you have to fulfil your destiny. You can ignore it. However, if you don't fulfil your life's journey, you might have to come back in another life and fulfil it later.

QUESTION: What happens if you DO fulfil your life's journey? What choices do you get when you cross over?

LORAINE: I suppose you could still choose to come back again. You might have other lessons to learn. I feel that we do choose our parents, and our children choose us. We have loads of choices. Some spirits become a spirit guide. And some on the other side help other souls heal from their trauma or emotional damage. In essence, they become a spirit guide for spirits.

QUESTION: Do you have other spirit guides besides Ramos?

LORAINE: I do. While Ramos is my main gate-keeper, there are others that show up from time to time. My great-grandmother Lucy Emelia is one of my spirit guides. She has been with me since I was very young. I am not sure why Lucy Emelia did not become my main spirit guide, but I still get messages from her, although not as often as when I was younger. Now it's only about once a month.

I have been told by four separate mediums that they see Doris Stokes around me. She was a well-known clairvoyant back in the 1980's who is gone now. But it seems she is also one of my spirit guides.

QUESTION: If people have psychic abilities, should they develop them?

LORAINE: It is a personal choice. People can open up to their talent and develop it further if they wish. But not everyone wants to. It's a personal choice to use it or not.

QUESTION: How can people develop their own clairvoyance?

LORAINE: I believe that everyone has psychic ability, to some degree. Some people choose to ignore it, or have left it behind with their childhood years. If you want to develop your psychic talents, I would suggest finding a teacher, a course, or a mentor that you feels right to you. If you don't feel good about it, leave the course or the teacher. Trust your instincts because as I've said before, your first thoughts are those that are guided by spirit. Those are the thoughts that will steer you in the right direction. Your second thoughts come from your own self, and those are not always the correct path for you. This is the best advice I can give you, whether it involves developing your talent or anything else.

QUESTION: What is it like on the other side?

LORAINE: When my heart stopped during surgery in 2008, I felt my body floating, and found myself in a tunnel of light. It was very peaceful and part of me wanted to stay there, although I knew I should return because of the kids. The doctors said I was only out for about seven minutes each time, so it wasn't a very lengthy experience.

However, a few years later I had a much longer experience that showed me what it was like on the other side.

In 2009 I was on holiday in Rome with my family, near the Coliseum, when all of a sudden, I felt very strange, as if I was in a black and white movie. I saw chariots and gladiators racing around engaged in violent sports. People were dying, women were screaming, and it was a really frightening experience because I wasn't able to control these visions or get them out of my head.

My husband Mark was very worried about me. We went back to our hotel and I asked Mark, who is trained in past life regression, to help me get into a meditative state so I could relax.

As soon as he did, I saw Ramos, clearer than I had ever seen him, and he took my hand. I felt myself being dragged up, as if I was taking a ride at the fair, but it was all very peaceful and calm. There was no tunnel and no white light that I could see.

The next thing I knew, I was standing by a large marble and gold building. Ramos told me that we were about to enter the "hospital." We went in, and there was beautiful, gentle music playing. It wasn't like a melody I can recall, but more like a peaceful soft wind.

The first "room" we went by was full of little children. They seemed very happy, all giggling and laughing. One little blonde boy, who identified himself as Stevie, touched my leg and said, "Tell Mummy I'm okay. You will talk to my mummy later."

In another side room there was one large "bed" that was divided into sections, each one cradling a very tiny soul, so small you could fit each one in your hand. They didn't speak as such, but I could understand them in a sort of mental communication.

The room was a healing chamber, and these tiny souls were the souls of premature babies who had died or had been aborted before delivery. I was told that sometimes a soul's path was to only touch the mother's womb before it needed to return back up here. Perhaps that was all that the mother needed. These tiny souls had limited experience of life, and had come here to this peaceful chamber to heal before moving on. As far as I could tell, there was no distinction between those who had died in the womb and those who had been terminated.

Another room held the souls of fully-formed people. These were adults who had done something they were ashamed of, such as taking their own life or having affairs. They were now very sorry, and needed a comforting place to heal.

Then Ramos told me we had to go somewhere else. As we passed down the corridor, I could feel we were approaching a horrible energy. I didn't want to go there, but Ramos said I needed to look in. I didn't want to, but I did. This room was full of angry souls, and I could feel their rage and total frustration as their screaming touched my mind. These souls had done terrible things during their lives, people like Hitler who had purposely caused misery. Trapped in this space with each other, all angry and bitter, they were never to leave this awful place until they learned to overcome their pasts, abandon the hurtful part of their natures, and grow beyond it.

Ramos told me that this was the closest to "hell" I was ever going to see. He also told me that only one out of three of these souls would ever get better. I was very glad when we left that horrible place.

Then I found we were by a big door. It didn't open, but somehow, Ramos and I moved to the other side. The colours here were very intense and beautiful, not like anything I have ever seen. And as I saw souls go about their business, I could "hear" their thoughts. I asked one soul what he was doing, and he told me he was looking after the flowers. He was a gardener in his life, and he had not stopped gardening, even on the other side. He said that the people on Earth still had a lot to learn about taking care of the land.

In the distance, I could see people I recognized. It was my mum, my gran, and my grandad. They were waving at me, not for me to come over to them, but just to say hello.

I wanted to go over there to them, but Ramos stopped me. I couldn't believe it. My own spirit guide, preventing me from being with the people up here that I loved the most. I argued with him, and told him he was nasty for keeping me back. He said they were too far, and if I went all the way over there, I wouldn't be able to go back to the earth plane. At that point, I really didn't want to go back to my life, I wanted the peacefulness of this other world.

But Ramos dragged me back, and I woke up in my hotel room with Mark beside me, looking worried as he huddled over me. He said I had been out for forty-five minutes. In all that time he had been trying to wake me up, but there was nothing he could do, and he had feared I wasn't ever going to come back.

But I did. And when I awoke, my visions of chariots and past times were gone.

A week later, after I returned to England from my vacation, I did a show where an audience member asked me what it was like on the other side. While I have been asked that question before, I never had a very full answer. When my heart stopped after my miscarriage, I was only out for about seven minutes each time, so I wasn't involved in the experience very long. But this time, I was "there" a lot longer. Maybe I needed to learn more and get that glimpse of the other side so I could pass it on.

And there was something else I needed to pass on, because later that same day, I read for a woman and brought her a message, a special request from the son that she lost, a little blonde boy named Stevie.

Chapter 12

BEYOND WORDS, BEYOND WORLDS

I saw Loraine one month later in a completely different setting. It was October of 2010 and the event was a private party. Loraine came that evening to a house to conduct private readings for the guests. The one-on-one sessions were to be held in a separate room, away from the other guests to guarantee privacy. Since a typical reading takes twenty minutes, in an evening stretch of four hours, she can do a dozen readings.

The guests arrived at the house unsure what to expect. Most had never met Loraine before. I had already seen her in action, but in this different setting, even I wasn't sure what would happen. Some people were nervous, some doubtful. Then one by one, they filed into the room set aside for the readings.

The first person to get read returned with a look of pure wonder. The second one emerged with his face glistening with tears of joy.

But the third guest raced out of the room, her skin flushed, and rushed up to me, asking, "Does Loraine have a secret dimmer switch behind her back?"

"What are you talking about?" I asked, completely thrown by her question.

"The ceiling lights were going crazy," my friend told me, "going up and down and off and on."

"There's no dimmer switch in there," said a young man named Saavik. "I installed those lights myself and wired them into the crawl space above the ceiling. I know every inch of that crawl space, and the only switch for those recessed lights is the on-off switch on the wall. There's no dimmer in that room."

He was right, those lights have never been on any sort of a dimmer system. I should know because Saavik is my handy-man, and the private home where this event was held was my house.

Later on in the evening, I went into the room to bring Loraine some dinner and give her a break. Once I had entered the room, the lights above us started flashing off and on, sometimes fast like a flicker, sometimes going bright to dark slowly, without anyone being anywhere near the light switch. It was the strangest welcome I have ever had, and especially so since it was happening in my own house.

After a few moments of this, the lights went back to normal, although it happened several more times that night during the readings.

One woman, Kate, initially wasn't sure she would have a reading. When she finally decided to have one, Loraine gave her a powerful message from her grandmother. Kate told Loraine that she wanted to believe her, that this message was really coming from her grandmother. But since the message was so near and dear to her heart, she just needed more proof.

As soon as Kate said this, the unexplained light show began. Others had similar experiences, with the lights beginning their peculiar display often at the same moment a particular loved one came through.

When Loraine finished her last session and stood up, signalling that the readings were done, the lights remained on and stayed on, completely finished with their mischievous activity. The bulbs were not burned out and the wiring was fine, as if it had never occurred. I watched that room over the next several weeks, but the lights were through with acting on their own. It only happened that night, in that one room, during about half of the readings. Not everyone was treated to a dancing light display.

Of those that were, some were intrigued, some amazed. But by this point, after everything I had already seen, I thought I was beyond being shocked by anything that might happen when Loraine goes to work.

I was wrong.

Near the end of the 2010, I got one final reading from Loraine that year. During the session, she told me she was "seeing" a baby girl. She had said this once before, on my very first reading when I had met her back in 2007. When Loraine had brought up the baby girl back then, I wasn't ready to discuss it. I didn't even acknowledge it at the time and had not brought it up with her since.

But by now, I had observed Loraine in action long enough to trust the messages, and the process. So when she brought up the baby girl again, the infant who was in the spirit world, this time I was ready to deal with the fact that Loraine was talking about *my* baby daughter, my first child, who was born with a damaged heart.

Her heart was so weak that she needed major surgery to repair it. When she was a month old, we took her to Seattle to some of the best doctors in the world, to have the open heart surgery required to save her life. The operation that was supposed to be finished before lunch ended up taking much longer. We waited in sickening dread as the minutes turned into hours, the hands of the clock relentlessly ticking our hopes away.

Then, miraculously, after six gruelling hours, the surgeon came out of the operating room and said that everything was fine. The operation was a success, the new heart valves and tubes were in place, her system had accepted them, and her heartbeat was strong. For the first time in her life, she had a pulmonary system as good as anyone else's and everything was working just fine.

But twenty minutes later, her heart stopped for no apparent reason, and they were unable to coax it to start again. So my little girl died right there in the hospital, after her system had been successfully repaired, and the doctors couldn't tell us why.

"Maybe," one said, "it was too much strain."

Whatever the reason, her tiny heart just gave up – *she* gave up. After we worked so hard to get her what she needed, and it was all fixed, that is when she left this world. When she left me.

So when Loraine brought up the baby girl this time, I knew exactly who she was talking about, and I said, "She chose to leave, didn't she?"

"Yes," said Loraine. "But they're telling me there's something you need to hear. You have to know that she accepted the job of being your daughter, knowing it would only be for a very short time. But she chose it anyway."

In that moment, something changed, a seismic tidal-wave shift in my deepest hidden-away core. Years of suppressed resentment melted away, baggage that I didn't even realize I had been carrying inside all that time until I saw the whole thing from this very different angle. In over twenty years, no one had been able to say anything remotely helpful about the situation, but now I realized something I had never considered before.

It was true that my daughter had left her life, and me. But at the same time, she had given up her chance at a long healthy life with someone else, just to be my daughter for a very brief time.

What a gift.

And it made me realize, first-hand, what a difference a handful of words, inspired words from the other side, could make. Because from that moment on, this new truth became a part of me, illuminating my path, every footstep, every view, every horizon, and clearing the way for a whole new acceptance.

And a richer peace.

I still enjoy watching people emerge from Loraine's shows or a private reading, after receiving a message of searing importance.

After experiencing this for myself, it is just as gratifying to see when someone else gets *one of those* readings, the kind that touches the soul on the deepest of levels, and in the most positive way.

As science tells us, matter and energy do not cease to exist, they are merely transformed. In a similar vein, most of the world's religions tell us that the soul does not end upon death.

For me, Loraine confirms these things, and validates them in a style that is all her own. From everything I have seen, I can only conclude that she is an amazing conduit, not only of messages from beyond, or in connecting us with loved ones we thought we had lost, or even resolving issues we didn't know that we had. She also reveals that we are more than what we can see. And if we open our eyes and our ears and our hearts to the process, and embrace the bonds of love that never end, we can realize that neither will we.

APPENDIX I

Below are excerpts of comments and testimonials from Loraine's website guest book, posted during the year of 2010. As Loraine has often said, she can not control the messages that come through, she can only trust that what she receives is what the person needs to hear. You can read the comments in their entirety and view the current postings at: *www.LoraineReesMedium.com*

"Thank you for the amazing reading you gave me. Your accuracy was mind-blowing."

"My mum and myself had a reading tonight and we are over the moon. Totally amazed and not even letting Mum pay for her reading shows me you are true, honest, and one hundred percent full of compassion. Truly a once in a lifetime experience."

"Amazing funny lady. The messages from beyond were a million and one percent amazing."

"Totally the best medium I have ever seen. Blew us away."

"I went to see [[a well-known medium]] and was painfully saddened and disappointed and came away feeling ripped-off. I was reluctant to pay another ten pounds of my hard-earned cash to see Loraine but I went and within ten minutes, Loraine had me in tears and was spot on."

"Good news! Loraine told me my daughter was pregnant. I asked her the sex and she said one of each. Well, just to confirm -- Lisa is having twins. Too early to find out the sex but watch this space."

"Well-spent. The best tenner ever to see Loraine's show on Friday for the M.S. charity."

"Thank you, Loraine, for the message from my mum. It meant the world to me. You are beautiful inside and out."

"I have been to five or six shows since Tom died but Loraine is the only one who got him. I am your biggest fan for life."

"Had the most beautiful reading ever."

"Amazing reading. Thank you, thank you. I always feel so much after a reading."

"I saw Loraine at the Cambridge MBS event and she's healed my aching heart."

"After seeing Loraine last night, she has changed my life forever."

"Went to see Loraine's show last week. My husband came through, sorry for taking his own life. Then he went on to say he knew about the new guy I'm seeing and all I do is push him away. So true! I can move on with my life now."

"I had a reading with you a few weeks ago. I asked you not to tell me anything bad about my disabled daughter and you did. You told me she had a few good years yet. I don't know how to cope with this."

"Would recommend everybody to have this experience at least once."

"Just gets better every time I see her."

"Didn't understand what you meant at my last reading but it's all come true. Sadly, it wasn't good but it was time for it to happen. Can't wait to have my next reading."

APPENDIX II

THE BRENTWOOD VIDEO

The videotape we shot of Loraine's medium demonstration at the Brentwood Mind Body Soul Exhibition, filmed on the 27th of March 2010, is available for viewing at the following site: **www.MaryRoss.org**

This site contains links for twelve roughly five-minute clips, in sequence, that cover the entire show. As you will see from these video clips, this film was not professionally edited (we couldn't even get the electronic date right) but was only shot as an aid to me in preparing this book. However, I have decided to make it available on the web for the readers of this book and anyone else who might be interested. While I believe the book makes a good attempt at portraying Loraine's abundant psychic talent, it falls short of adequately conveying the humour and warmth that infuse every one of her public appearances, which have to be seen to be fully appreciated.

INDEX

ABOUT THE AUTHOR

Dr. Mary Ross was born in New York and moved to England in 2001. A trained scientist with a master's degree in earth science, in her doctoral research, in education, she explored ways of combining right brain with left brain modes of thinking in order to help university students achieve their potential, with dramatic results.

After meeting Loraine Rees, Mary examined Loraine's practice over a period of four years. The result is this book in which she uses her observational skills and questioning mind to create an insightful portrayal of a modern clairvoyant at work.

Lightning Source UK Ltd.
Milton Keynes UK
UKOW05f2215080813

215098UK00001B/275/P